Méribel & the 3 Valleys
A Mad Dog Ski resort guide

Second edition 2008
Published by Mad Dog Ski
maddogski.com

Mad Dog Ski
Méribel & the 3 Valleys
Second edition 2008

Published by Mad Dog Ski
Maps © Mad Dog Ski

Edited by: Gaby de Pace and Tory Dean
Design: David Marshall
Artwork & print: Etrinsic print management

ISBN 978-0-9551215-1-7

A catalogue record of this book is available at the British Library.

Mad Dog Ski, PO Box 6321, Bournemouth, BH1 9ED, UK
info@maddogski.com
maddogski.com
+44 (0) 845 054 2906

All rights reserved. No part of this publication may be reproduced or transmitted in any form or by any means, electronically or mechanically, including photography, recording or any information storage or retrieval system without prior written permission from the publisher. No part of this publication may be used in any form of advertising, sales promotion or publicity without prior written permission from the publisher.

Contents

Don't miss our handy quick reference sections...

Resort map 6

The piste map 88

Lift pass prices 29

Live music 80

Our favourite restaurants.................... 71

Our favourite bars........... 81

Our favourite mountain restaurants.................... 87

About Mad Dog Ski

About this book 2
Snow & weather reports 3
About our researchers 3

About Méribel

The resort 5
Resort map...........................6
Ski area overview 10

Planning your trip

Getting there......................13
Where to stay.....................14
Useful numbers
& websites 17

On the piste

The ski area........................23
Boarders.............................26
Off-piste & heli-skiing..........26
Cross-country 26
Beginners...........................27
Lift passes 27
Weather.............................29
Safety 31
Ski & snowboard schools 32
Equipment hire...................33
Piste rankings.....................34
Day trips 54

Food and drink

Savoyard food & drink................66
Vegetarian options 68
Budget meals & take-aways.......69
Reading our reviews 70
Resort restaurants 71
Après-ski & nightlife..................79
Mountain restaurants................86

Other things to do

Non-skiing activities................107
Shopping..................................115

Children

Accommodation 123
Childcare 127
Ski schools 127
Lift passes 127
Activities 130
Restaurants 131

The list 132

Maps

Resort..6
Resort restaurants & bars 72
Mountain restaurants.................88

About Mad Dog resort guides and how they'll make a real difference to your holiday.

What you'll find in this chapter

About this book..................2
Snow and weather updates..................3
About our researcher..................3

About Mad Dog Ski

My time in the mountains used to be restricted to one or two precious weeks a year. Each winter, I would arrive with my ski buddies, eager to get on the slopes as soon as possible, indulge in some good après-ski and ensure we had somewhere decent to re-fuel at lunchtimes. All too often, this precious information comes the day before you're heading home.

During my first season as a thirty-something chalet host, I realised I wasn't alone in my quest for reliable information. Week after week guests would ask the same questions; where should they ski, where were the best mountain restaurants, how do you get there? Mad Dog Ski was born.

Everything in our books and on maddogski.com is researched by skiers and boarders who know the resort they are writing about inside out.

Not only that, but we are passionate about helping our readers get the most out of their holiday from the moment they arrive to the moment they leave. We want you to love the resort and the mountains as much as we do.

With Mad Dog Ski, we always give you our independent view – extra special places and people are shown throughout this book as 'Mad Dog favourites'. If our taste varies from yours, or if you find places we haven't, please write to us or email us at **info@maddogski.com**.

Enjoy the mountain!

Kate Whittaker
Founder, Mad Dog Ski

About this book

Mad Dog books are designed to be most use when you actually get to Méribel. To keep them small enough for your ski jacket pocket, we've stuck to just the essentials. For the full lowdown on planning your trip (your travel options, where to stay and that kind of thing) check out **maddogski.com.** If you can't find what you're looking for or have a particularly tricky question, check out the Ask Mad Dog area at the bottom of the homepage where you can email us – we love a challenge!

We're not perfect!

Whilst we make every effort to get things right, places, prices and opening times do change from season to season. If you spot an error or if you simply have a different opinion to us, get in contact as **info@maddogski.com.**

Prices

All prices are based on the 2006/7 season. Prices for food, drink and services in resort are given in euros (€).

Skier or boarder?

Throughout this book, 'skiing' and 'skier' are used as interchangeable terms for 'riding' and 'snowboarder'. No offence is intended – it just helps make our books smaller.

Telephone numbers

All numbers are prefixed by their French dialling code. Landlines in Méribel are prefixed by the code '04 79' (so +33 (0)4 79…) whilst French mobiles start with an '06' (+33 (0)6…).

To call France from the UK, dial '+33' and drop the first '0' of the French number. From France to the UK, dial '+44' and omit the first '0' of the UK number.

There are public telephones that accept phone cards (available from a Tabac > 122) throughout resort. If you plan to use your UK mobile before leaving the UK, remember that you pay to receive calls as well as to make them, so text messages are often a cheaper way to stay in touch.

Snow and weather reports

For up-to-date information about the resort, **maddogski.com** has snow reports, weather forecasts and webcams for Méribel. You can also sign up for our regular newsletter.

Tell us what you think

Tell us about your favourite (or least favourite) places in Méribel at **maddogski.com.** Simply check out the entry under Méribel and 'Add your review'.

About our researcher

Gina Greenall
After seven winters living and working in Méribel, it's still one of Gina's favourite places to be. Having worked a variety of jobs, many never to be repeated – two trips in a day to Geneva airport and guests arriving at 5.30am – she has concluded that working in winter is overrated!

Best restaurant: Le Tremplin – great steak and very friendly staff ➤ 76.
Best après-ski: The Rond Point for the liveliest après-ski in town and a great ski down in the dark after a few toffee vodkas! ➤ 95.
Favourite lunch stop: Les Crêtes – small, French and great food ➤ 93.
Best run: Mont Vallon especially the Combe du Vallon – the best and probably the longest run in the valley ➤ 38.

SKI CHALETS

Traditional Chalets
Catered & Self-catered

meribel, motteret & many more fantastic resorts...

Quintessential alpine chalets with breathtaking views and sunny balconies in idyllic mountain settings.

Make your next skiing holiday a reality ...not just a dream!

www.chaletfinder.co.uk - 01453 766094

Méribel; the pretty resort in the middle of the Three Valleys where Brits love to party.

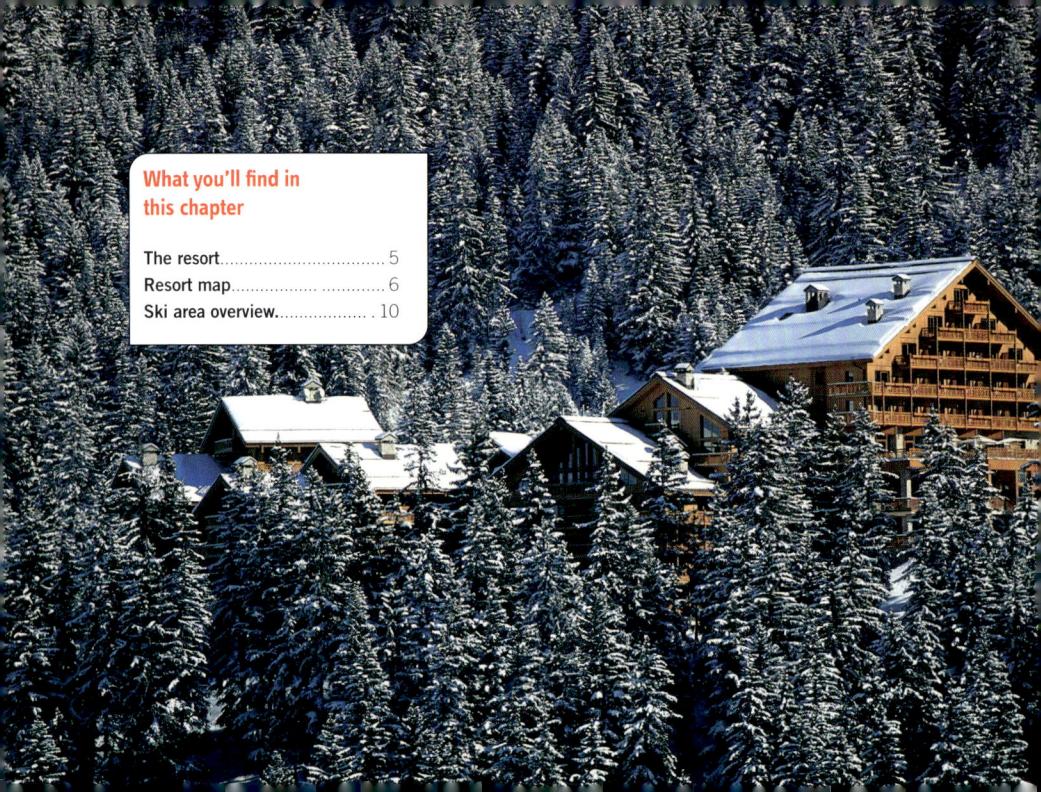

What you'll find in this chapter

The resort.................... 5
Resort map.................. 6
Ski area overview............. 10

About Méribel

Charming chalets, fantastic slopes, lively après-ski... It's easy to see why people fall in love with Méribel and come back season after season.

Like neighbouring Courchevel, Méribel isn't a budget resort. The sheer number of different companies that offer accommodation does however mean you can often get a bargain, if you are happy to travel outside school holidays and can book last minute. The Three Valleys ski domain is vast but, just even on its own, Méribel offers a wide variety of slopes, including some charming tree lined runs. And, because of the resort's location, you can follow the sun all day. As for après-ski, Méribel is legendary. You'll find great bars, live-music venues and nightclubs – all evidence of its reputation as a party place.

Of course, no resort is perfect. Not everyone wants to be surrounded by skiers from the UK (we account for around 35% of foreign visitors without including the hordes of seasonal workers). The sun can make the slopes slushy in the afternoons and the chalet-style accommodation makes parts of the resort feel rather sprawled out.

The resort lies in the Les Allues valley and is made up of four main villages – Méribel, Mottaret, Méribel-Village and Les Allues. These range in height from 1100m (Les Allues) to 1750m (Mottaret), and access to the ski area extends as far down as Brides-les-Bains (600m) via the Olympe gondola.

Méribel

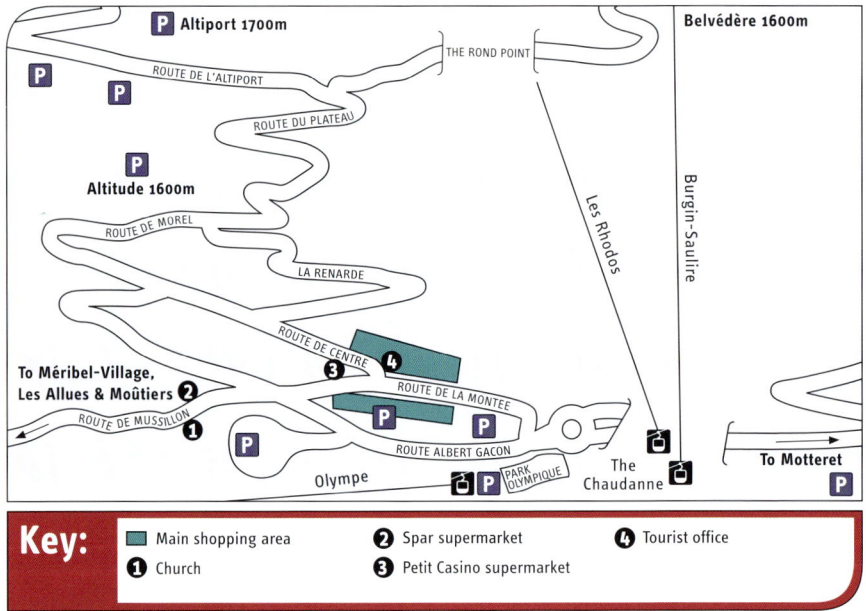

ake off this season with the whole family

ki Cuisine has become firmly established as one of Méribel's
ading chalet operators. Our knowledge and experience
 this premier resort coupled with a superb portfolio
 chalets and our renowned service ensures
at we can offer you a holiday
perience to remember.

- Warm, friendly atmosphere
- Hand picked chalets & staff
- Professional a la carte service
- Child friendly chalets and menus
- Fully qualified Nannies
- English speaking Ski Instructors
- Ski schools for children
- Over 600km of pistes

ki Cuisine

ww.skicuisine.co.uk   Tel: 01702 589543   Email: info@skicuisine.co.uk

For most people, Méribel is considered the heart of the resort although, at 1450m, it isn't the highest. Purpose-built but with a strict code forbidding high-rise properties, it is a vision of wooden chalets and home to most of the best bars and restaurants.

The village itself is made up of various satellite areas, some of which are a walk or bus ride from the centre. On the plus side, you can opt for cheaper accommodation away from the centre. UK holiday companies often have chalets in these areas, including Mussillon, Le Plateau, 1600 and Morel. Here, accommodation is more likely to be ski in, ski out, with some good restaurants nearby. We recommend Le Rond Point (> 83), fantastic for early après-ski.

Mottaret

Thought of as Méribel's rather plain sister due to its high-rise look, Mottaret is higher up the valley (1750m), so has a better chance of holding onto its snow. It's better placed for exploring the Three Valleys and there's a

Getting around: Méribel's main landmarks and areas

- **The Chaudanne:** the main lift area
- **The main square:** here you'll find the tourist office, Post Office and La Taverne bar
- **Parc Olympique:** the sports centre near the Chaudanne
- **Route de la Montée:** lined with shops and restaurants, this road links the main square to the Chaudanne

> **Méribel at a glance**
> - Access to 600km of marked and interconnecting pistes
> - Access to 200 ski lifts across the Three Valleys
> - 14 villages and hamlets between Mottaret (1750m) and Les Allues (1100m)
> - 600 snow canons – 1662 in the Three Valleys
> - 23 piste bashers – 76 in the Three Valleys
> - Runs from 3000m to 1100m
> - More than 10,000 hectares off-piste
> - Over 50 mountain restaurants in the Three Valleys

higher proportion of ski in, ski out accommodation.

The focus of the village is the main lift area. Here, you'll see a large wooden building which houses the tourist office and cinema. Based nearby, there's L'Ecole de Ski Français (ESF), the lift pass office and a number of restaurants.

Generally, après-ski in Mottaret is fairly low-key. Most people head to Méribel for a night out as it's only 10 minutes away by bus. Ski access is via the pretty **Truite,** which is also good for sledging after the lifts close.

Méribel-Village

At 1400m, this compact little village has pretty much all you need for a more peaceful Alpine holiday. There's plenty of chalet accommodation (much of it ski in, ski out), a supermarket and baker, plus the famous Lodge du Village – or LDV as locals call it – a lively après-ski bar and restaurant. Entrance to the Three Valleys isn't as good as from other areas, but with easy access to the practice runs around the Altiport, the village is popular with beginners.

Don't leave Méribel without...

- Taking a flight over the Three Valleys (> 110)
- Having a mountain lunch at the wonderfully cosy Adray Télébar (> 93)
- Hiring a guide and heading off-piste (> 26)
- Taking the kids to the water slides (> 130)
- Skiing all three valleys in one day (> 54)
- Catching a live band at Le Rond Point (> 95)
- Spending the night dancing at Dicks Tea Bar (> 82)
- Renting a skidoo in Mottaret (> 111)
- Treating yourself to a massage at your chalet (> 108)

Les Allues

Although small and set low down in the valley (1100m), Les Allues has an endearing traditional feel not found in the other villages. The pretty stone buildings and chalets fan out from the central area, which is made up of the town hall, Hotel La Croix Jean-Claude, a ski hire shop, supermarket and a few restaurants. Quite a few of the chalets are privately owned which gives the village a unique 'local' atmosphere.

Méribel is 15-20 minutes away by bus or you can catch the Olympe gondola to the Chaudanne.

The skiing

The Three Valleys (made up of Méribel, Courchevel and Val Thorens) has some of the most extensive and impressive skiing in the world – America's six largest resorts would fit into the area. The pistes around Méribel are wonderfully sunny however, in snow-sparse times, you also have the option of heading to Courchevel's primarily north-facing slopes, or to Val Thorens' higher pistes. For more on the skiing > 23.

three*vallee*transfers

Airport transfers to Les Trois Vallees.

Geneva. Chambery. Lyon. Grenoble. Moutiers Station.
Private and Shared minibus transfers.
www.3vt.co.uk

UK: +44 (0)1782 644420 / France: +33 (0)603 367927

Helping you to **plan your trip;** your travel options, where to stay and useful tips.

What you'll find in this chapter

Getting there 13
Where to stay 14
Useful numbers & websites 17

Our books are designed to be a handy companion in resort. To keep them pocket-sized, we put the most up-to-date planning information and tips on maddogski.com. This chapter gives you a simple overview together with useful websites and contacts.

Getting there

If you're arranging your own travel (rather than booking a package holiday) you have several options. You can fly to Geneva, Lyon St Exupéry, Grenoble and Chambéry airports. Chambéry and Grenoble are closer but Geneva has the best track record of staying open in bad weather.

Remember to check ski and board baggage charges which can significantly push up the price of a 'cheap' flight. For up-to-date baggage information, check out **maddogski.com**.

The snow trains run by Eurostar and Rail Europe are a more eco-friendly route to the Alps with Eurostar carbon neutral from

maddogski.com

- Travel advice, including details of getting to France (self-drive, trains, airlines and ferries) and how to get to resort once you arrive (airport transfer companies, car hire and buses)
- Accommodation, including reviews of chalets, hotels and apartments
- Everything else you need to know about before you book your trip, from winter sports insurance to the latest snow reports

2007. Eurostar runs direct services to Moûtiers from St Pancras or Ashford taking around eight hours. Choose an overnight train on Friday or Saturday, or daytime on Saturday. Although pricier (from £220) than low-cost airlines, the journey is relaxing and you avoid lengthy transfers. For a livelier experience, start your holiday early with Rail Europe's infamous party snow train (see opposite).

For overnight travellers, it's unlikely your accommodation will be ready when you arrive, so you'll need to arrange somewhere to store your bags while you get on the slopes.

Regular buses run from Geneva airport (from €150 round trip) and Moûtiers train station (from €24). Whilst there are transfer links from other airports, these can be inconsistent and often mean lengthy waits at the airport, so car hire or airport transfers are the best options.

For a door-to-door service, the English-speaking private transfer companies or taxis are a good option (especially for early morning flights). They're not even that expensive, particularly for larger groups (> 19).

If you're planning on driving from the UK, it should take around 12 hours to reach the Three Valleys once you arrive at your French port. French motorways are a lot emptier than the UK, although expect to pay between €50-60 in toll fees, either in cash or on credit card (not debit card).

Remember as well that the final approaches to resort can see huge tailbacks and delays in high season.

Where to stay

Méribel can accommodate up to 30,000 sleepy skiers a night so you'll easily find somewhere to suit you and your budget. Although there is a selection of hotels and self-catering apartments, the focus here is on catered chalet holidays. The chalets come in all sizes, but tend to sleep around 10-16 people. If your group isn't big enough to fill one, you'll end up sharing (and making new friends!). Visit **maddogski.com** for a full list of our favourites.

Check where in the resort your

fast track to méribel with the snow train

Why not take the Rail Europe's Snow Train? Depart Friday night from either St Pancras or Ebbsfleet International on Eurostar and connect with the overnight service in Paris. You'll arrive fresh for a full day of skiing on Saturday morning. Return the following Saturday night.

- Enjoy 2 extra days on the slopes!
- Comfortable, flat-bed sleeping accommodation
- Stops at 6 stations serving 25 resorts
- Bar and disco carriages
- Skis and snowboards go free
- Short, easy transfers to resort
- Bi-lingual reps on board

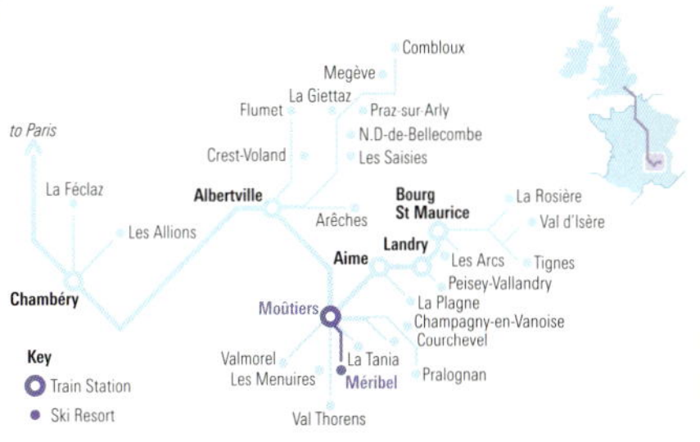

return from

£219 for Méribel take the Snow Train to Moûtiers

for more information and to book
call **0844 848 4062** or visit www.raileurope.co.uk

accommodation is before booking and also ask whether your holiday company offers a shuttle service to and from the slopes. About Méribel (➤ 5) tells you more about the different villages in the resort.

If it's a hotel you're after, Méribel itself offers the most choice. **La Chaudanne** (chaudanne.com) is a family-run hotel in the centre of the resort. It's right next to the slopes and has impressive facilities, including a wonderful heated outdoor pool. **Le Yéti** (hotel-yeti.com) is a good mid-range all-rounder close to the Rond-Point.

If you're on a tight budget, try the central **Hotel Le Roc** (lataverne-meribel.com) above the popular après-ski hangout La Taverne. Up in Mottaret the luxurious **Mont-Vallon** (hotel-montvallon.com) could hardly be more convenient for skiing the Three Valleys and has a wonderfully

Airport transfer times

Airport	kms to Méribel	Approx transfer time by road	Airlines
Chambéry	101	1.5 hours	Flybe, Flyglobespan, Jet2
Geneva	134	3 hours	Air France, bmi baby, BA, easyJet, Flybe, Flyglobespan, Jet 2, Swiss Air
Grenoble	167	2.5 hours	BA, easyJet, Ryanair, Thomsonfly
Lyon St Exupéry	178	3.5 hours	Air France, bmi baby, BA, easyJet

simple mountain style. If you're looking for a calmer, 'French' holiday, check out **La Croix Jean-Claude** in the centre of Les Allues, or stay piste-side in the rooms above the lovely **Adray Télébar** mountain restaurant (telebar-hotel.com).

Self-caterers can choose between chalets or, more commonly, apartments. The tourist office website, **meribel.com**, is a good starting point for ideas, or see our website.

If you're too tired to cook after a day on the slopes, **>** 69 take-aways and **>** 73 restaurants.

Useful numbers and websites

Airports

Chambéry
T + 33 (0)4 79 54 43 54
W chambery.aeroport.fr

Grenoble
T +33 (0)4 76 65 48 48
W grenoble.aeroport.fr

Geneva
T +41 (0)2 27 17 71 11
W gva.ch

Lyon St Exupéry
T +33 (0)4 26 00 70 07
W lyonairport.com

Airlines

Air France
T +44 (0)870 142 4343
W airfrance.co.uk

British Airways
T +44 (0)870 850 9850
W britishairways.com

bmibaby
T +44 (0)871 224 0224
W bmibaby.com

easyJet
T +44 (0)905 521 0905
W easyjet.com

Flybe
T +44 (0)871 522 6100
W flybe.com

Planning your trip

Flyglobespan
T +44 (0)871 271 0415
W flyglobespan.com

Jet2
T +44 (0)871 226 1737
W jet2.com

Ryanair
T +44 (0)871 246 0000
W ryanair.com

Swiss
T +44 (0)845 601 0956
W swiss.com

Thomsonfly
T +44 (0)870 165 0079
W thomsonfly.com
Doncaster flights to Geneva

Trains
Eurostar
T +44 (0)870 518 6186
W eurostar.com

Rail Europe
T +44 (0)8708 371 371
W raileurope.co.uk

SNCF
T +33 (0) 892 35 35 35
W voyages-sncf.com

Buses
Altibus
T +44 (0)820 32 03 68
(only active during winter)
W altibus.com
Chambéry, Geneva and Lyon

Satobus
Lyon St Exupéry
T +33 (0)4 27 00 70 07
W satobus-alps.com

Car hire
For details of parking and garages in Méribel (➤6).

Auto Europe
T +44 (0)800 358 1229
W auto-europe.co.uk

Avis
T +44 (0)844 581 0147
W avis.co.uk

Budget
T +44 (0)844 581 9998
W budget.co.uk

easyCar
T +44 (0)8710 500 444
W easycar.co.uk

Europcar
T +44 (0)607 5000
W europcar.co.uk

Hertz
T +44 (0)844 8844
W hertz.co.uk

Holiday autos
T +44 (0)870 400 4461
W holidayautos.co.uk

Private transfers
ATS Airport Transfer Services
T +33 (0)4 50 53 63 97
W a-t-s.net

Threevalleetransfers
T +44 (0)1782 644420
W 3vt.co.uk

Taxis
G'Taxi
T +33 (0)6 09 52 78 52
W gtaximeribel.com

Méritaxis
T +33 (0)4 79 08 58 22
W meri-taxis.com

Taxi Jean Loup
T +33 (0)6 09 44 15 95
W taxijeanloup.com

Taxiphone Méribel
T +33 (0)4 79 08 65 10

Taxiphone Méribel-Mottaret
T +33 (0)4 79 00 44 29

Self-drive advice
Via michelin route planner
W viamichelin.co.uk

Driving abroad advice
W drivingabroad.co.uk

Ferries
Brittany Ferries
T +44 (0)870 366 5333
W brittany-ferries.com
From Poole, Portsmouth and Plymouth

P&O
T +44 (0)870 598 03 33
W poferries.com

From Dover and Portsmouth
Seafrance
T +44 (0)870 571 17 11
W seafrance.com

From Dover to Calais Alternatively **ferrybooker.com** and **cheap4ferries.com** offer a selection of fares from various companies.

Insurance
Insure and go
T +44 (0)870 901 3674
W insureandgo.com

Ski Club of Great Britain
T +44 (0)845 601 94227
W skiclubinsurance.co.uk

Ski Insurance
T +44 (0)870 755 6101
W ski-insurance.co.uk
You can also buy insurance with your lift pass ('carré neige' – €2.50 per day) which covers you for recovery from the mountain without having to prove you're insured or paying up front (should you be unfortunate enough to need it).

Lift passes
If you're very organised, you can buy your lift passes online (> 28).

Families
Travelling with children? We recommend booking childcare (> 127) before you arrive.

Tourist office
T +33 (0)4 79 00 50 00
> 143.
W meribel.com

This chapter aims to get you on the piste as quickly as possible. After all, it's why you're here.

What you'll find in this chapter

The ski area	23
Boarders	26
Off-piste & heli-skiing	26
Cross-country	26
Beginners	27
Lift passes	27
Weather	29
Safety	31
Ski & snowboard schools	32
Equipment hire	33
Piste rankings	34
Day trips	54

On the Piste

Welcome to one of the biggest ski areas in the world. While Paradiski (Les Arcs and La Plagne linked by the Vanoise Express) claims to be the largest, purists say the crown belongs to the Three Valleys, not least for the ease of skiing between the different areas.

In fact, the region has four valleys: Courchevel, Méribel, Val Thorens and Orelle (recently connected to the lift system). Skiing here is all about travelling – you'll be surprised at the distance you can cover in a day, discovering the valleys and pretty villages dotted around.

Méribel

Based in the centre of the Three Valleys, Méribel is an ideal resort for exploring the ski area. It's also perfect for early intermediates, with enough variety just within the Méribel valley itself to really hone their skills through the week.

Méribel is known for being one of the sunniest resorts in the Alps and is an absolute joy to ski in good snow. The only real downside is that on some parts of the slopes the heat tends to melt the top surface of snow, which then freezes overnight. This means slopes can be icy first thing and slushy in the afternoon. However, for the many fans of Méribel, this is a small price to pay for a great resort in a great location and maximum opportunity to come home with a healthy glow. When you're planning your day remember that the eastern slopes (nearest Courchevel) get the afternoon sun, so are usually best visited after lunch.

Mottaret is one of the best-placed villages for skiing the Three Valleys domain, being one lift away from Courchevel, St Martin and Les Menuires, and two from Val Thorens. Take the lovely tree-lined

maddogski.com

Truite to reach the Chaudanne (Méribel's central lift area). If you're staying in Les Allues and the snow is good you can ski home at the end of the day. Even Brides-les-Bains is accessible off-piste if you know what you're doing and there's enough snow.

Courchevel

1850 tends to be the destination for most people heading to Courchevel. From Méribel you'll probably pass through station and take one of three long green pistes run into La Croisette (the main lift area in 1850). However, don't miss **Creux** running between 1650 and 1850 ridges – one of the most enjoyable runs in Courchevel.

1650 is the furthest point of the Three Valleys and many never make it over here at all. Those that do find some great pistes which often keep their snow longer because there is less traffic.

1550, directly below 1850, probably isn't worth a detour for Méribel skiers, but if you come this far, two lifts connect back to 1850 (one directly into La Croisette).

La Tania (1350m) gets less sun than the other villages so the pistes can get icy, especially early in the morning, but don't let that put you off. Tree lined Folyères is one of the loveliest runs in the Alps, although it can feel more red than blue in icy conditions.

Le Praz, at 1300m, has two of the best blacks in the Three Valleys – **Jean Blanc** and **Jockeys** – as well as a long and challenging red (beginners are best taking the bus or the gondola into the resort).

Les Menuires and St Martin

Les Menuires – possibly the ugliest resort in the Alps – and St Martin, one of the prettiest, both have long, cruisy, confidence-boosting reds and blues. Particular favourites are **Pramint**, **Jérusalem**, and **Allemandes**. For blues don't miss Pelozet, Gros Tougne and Petit Creux.

Val Thorens

At 2300m this is the highest point of the Three Valleys, so don't

alpineanswers.co.uk

we make booking a ski holiday a pleasureable experience

The ultimate skiers and boarders website brings you up to date information on ski holidays, chalets, hotels, resorts, flexible breaks, late deals, snow reports and much more

For more information visit our website: **www.alpineanswers.co.uk**
or simply call us on: **020 7801 1080**

expect charming tree-lined runs. However, its altitude also helps it retain snow long after the other valleys have lost theirs so it's not all bad. Val Thorens also gives you access to the fourth valley Orelle – a must for good intermediates.

Boarders

Boarders – from total novice to advanced – will find plenty to keep them occupied. Where there are still drag lifts, there's usually an alternative. Our suggested day trips also detail these > 54.

If you don't like to walk, stay clear of these flatter slopes:

Méribel

- Boulevard de le Loze
- The last section of Truite
- There are two flattish sections on Lac de la Chambre
- Ours
- Sizerin – too flat even for skiers
- Villages

Courchevel

- Middle section of Bellecôte
- Last section of Col de la Loze
- Last section of Indiens

Val Thorens

- The feeder path from Béranger
- Névés

Les Menuires

- The first section of Gros Tougne
- Sections of Biolley

Snowparks

There are two snowparks in Méribel. The main one is next to the Plattières 2 lift and the smaller park is next to Grives. The snowpark in Courchevel 1850 is at the bottom of the Plantrey chairlift.

Off-piste and heli-skiing

Unless you're an experienced skier and know the area well, you should

Cross-country

There's an extensive network of cross-country skiing routes throughout Méribel and Courchevel. Get details and maps from the tourist office (> 143).

only ski off-piste with an instructor or mountain guide. All ski schools offer off-piste instruction and guiding, conditions allowing.

'Les Trois Vallées hors piste/off-piste' by Phillippe Baud and Benoît Loucel is a good source for off-piste. (Published by Guide Vamos and available in newsagents in resort).

Heli-skiing is banned in France but you can arrange to fly into nearby Italy or Switzerland with the **Bureau des Guides** (guides-courchevel-meribel.com).

ESF also offer off-piste guiding, ski touring and heli-skiing through the **Ecole de Hors Piste de l'ESF** (>32).

Beginners

ZEN areas (Zones d'Evolution des Novices) are wide and well protected pistes designed for beginners and families:

Méribel/Mottaret
ZEN du Rossignol

Courchevel 1850
ZEN du Practice. Rolling carpet lift (specifically for beginners)
ZEN de Pralong

Courchevel 1650
ZEN du Mickey

Le Praz
ZEN de l'Envolée
Once you're comfortable on the above, try these:

Blanchot: take Golf and then Altiport
Boulevard de la Loze: from the top of the Loze chair. This one isn't for boarders as it's too flat
Forêt: catch the rope drag next to the bottom of the Altiport lift
Lapin: from the top of the Golf chairlift from Méribel-Village
Martre: from the first station of Plattières. The last (and steepest) section into Mottaret gets busy at the end of the day
Rhodos: at the top of the Rhodos lift
Truite: runs from Mottaret to Méribel

Lift passes

Each village has a lift pass office (> 28). Photos are no longer required (except for season passes) but to qualify for the discounts, under 14s and over 60s will need proof of age.

As well as Méribel-only or a full Three Valleys pass, the lift company has options designed for families and beginners (> 127, **meribel.net** or the lift offices in resort). A Three Valley pass is best if you plan to leave the valley more than twice (remembering that high winds might shut the linking lifts). Beginners are usually fine with a Méribel-only pass and you can always buy daily upgrades if necessary. Absolute beginners may not need a pass for the first day – check with your ski school.

Online lift passes
Buy your pass online at least 10 days before your trip. You can collect it when you arrive or have it delivered to your hotel or chalet. Go to the 'skiing area' section of **meribel.net**. Passes can be kept from year to year and recharged.

Olympic lift passes
Six day plus passes include a day pass for Val d'Isère/Tignes, Les Arcs/La Plagne, Pralognan-La-Vanoise and Les Saisies (during the period your pass is valid for). You need to collect your pass at the central lift office in the relevant resort.

Lift pass offices
The main lift pass office is in the Tougnète lift station at the Chaudanne. You'll find other offices in Mottaret, the Rond-Point, Altiport and Méribel-Village. Minimum opening hours are 9am to 4.30pm (later in high season).

Adult lift pass prices (in €) for the 2007/8 season

No. of days	Méribel*	Three Valleys	Pedestrian**
1	37	36	15
2	73	44	24
3	108	130	32
4	136	170	38
5	162	203	44
6	178	220	50
7	200	261	
Half day	30	36	

*Courchevel to Three Valleys upgrade is €20 a day.
**Pedestrian passes cover all lifts and bus services in Méribel and Courchevel (except the Pass'montagne services). You can also buy one trip passes for €6 – trips down are free.

Lift closing times
Lift closing times are listed on the piste map and change in early February. Bad weather can also cause early lift closures.

Emergency telephone numbers
See the inside front over or a piste map. In you are involved in an accident, call piste security and give your location as precisely as you can.

If on a piste, it is a good idea to stand your skis or board in the snow above the victim to warn people coming down the hill, particularly if you are below a ridge or around a corner.

Weather
maddogski.com has weather forecasts and snow reports so you can keep an eye on the snowfall before you arrive in resort. Local radio stations give daily reports; Radio R' Méribel, 97.9 and 98.9fm,

Avalanche!

Whilst Méribel has automated explosive systems to prevent avalanches, the danger cannot be completely averted and every year people die on the mountain.

Speed is of the essence if you are caught in an avalanche. If the victim is alive after the initial impact there is an 80% chance of survival if rescued in the first 12 minutes, after 15 minutes the probability of a successful rescue drops dramatically. Your best chance of survival is to be rescued by someone in your own group, so we advise off-piste skiers carry a transceiver, shovel and probe.

Although manufacturers claim that mobile phones cause only minimum interference with transceiver signals, it's safer to switch off your mobile whilst off-piste.

The daily avalanche risk is shown clearly with flags and ratings on a scale of 1-5 throughout the Three Valleys. If in doubt, ask a piste security employee (dressed in black and yellow).

Avalanche risk report

T +33 (0)8 92 68 10 20 (€0.34 per minute)

W avalanches.org

Avalanche warning flags

1-2

Yellow
Limited risk

3-4

Black/yellow chequered flag
High risk

5

Black flag
Very high risk

Safety

Travelling at high speed is one of the great attractions of skiing but with it comes an element of danger.

Most accidents are caused by collisions; it is relatively easy for adult skiers to achieve speeds of over 50kph, even children can quite easily reach 45kph. Be aware of others and make sure you follow the piste rules.

Rules of the piste

1. Respect – do not endanger or prejudice the safety of others
2. Control – ski in control, adapting your speed and manner to ability, conditions and traffic. Give way to slower skiers
3. Choice of route – the uphill skier must choose his route so he does not endanger the skiers below
4. Overtaking – allowed left or right, above or below but always leave sufficient space for the overtaking skier
5. Entering and starting a run – look both up and down the piste before you head off
6. Stopping on the piste – avoid stopping at narrow or low visibility areas. Always stop at the edge of the piste rather than in the middle and make sure that you can be easily seen by approaching skiers
7. Climbing – if you have to walk up or down the piste, do so at the edge and ensure neither you nor your equipment are a danger to anyone else
8. Signs and markings – respect the information given about pistes and the weather
9. Accidents – if you witness an accident, you must give assistance, particularly by alerting piste security
10. Identification – if you are involved in or witness an accident, you must provide your identity to piste security if requested

The International Ski Federation (FIS) Code of Conduct

Radio Nostalgie Courchevel, 93.2fm.

Weather can change rapidly in the mountains with bright sunshine deteriorating into cold, low-visibility conditions. Make a habit of checking the weather reports posted in the tourist offices (➤ 143) and at main lifts (information boards show which runs are open, wind speed and avalanche risk). The tops of the right-hand piste markers are painted fluorescent orange to help you in poor visibility.

Ski and snowboard schools

Whilst the largest ski school is the ESF, the number of smaller international ski schools is growing. It is notoriously difficult to become an instructor under the French system, so you can be pretty confident of being taught by an excellent skier whichever school you choose. The main difference with the smaller British schools is (usually) a better command of English, and smaller class sizes. Many people think it's best to be taught by a native speaker of your own language.

If you are holidaying at a peak period (school holidays, Christmas and New Year), book your lessons as early as possible – especially for the British ski schools.

The prices we give here should be used as a guide only – check out individual websites for up-to-date details.

ESF

T +33 (0)4 79 08 60 31
W esf-meribel.com.
The Chaudanne.
Private tuition: half day from €102, full day €310
Group lessons: from €211 for five days
Max. group size: 12
The Rond-Point: +33 (0)4 79 08 89 42
Mottaret: +33 (0)4 79 00 49 49

In peak season there are 450 instructors who wear the familiar red ESF uniform in Méribel. Whilst you cannot guarantee fluency in English, the sheer number of instructors makes them very flexible in terms of lesson options and availability.

New Generation

T +33 (0)4 79 01 03 18
W skinewgen.com
The Chaudanne.
Instructors: eight
Private tuition: two hours from €155, full day from €435
Group lessons: from €175 for 10 hours
Max. group size: eight

New Gen is a British ski school with predominantly native English speakers. They have a good reputation for tuition. Classes revolve around helping you understand what you need to do so that you can continue improving after the lesson.

Magic Snowsports Academy (magic-meribel.com) is also worth a mention. Originally two separate ski schools – Magic in Motion and Ski Academy – they have combined to form one. They have a particularly good reputation with children.

Equipment hire

Most hire shops offer similar equipment at similar prices. We suggest using somewhere close to your accommodation. Alternatively, some companies, such as **Freeride**, will deliver. If you know what you want to hire you can often pre-book online.

Most shops offer their own inexpensive insurance. This saves you the hassle of paying up front should something happen to your skis or board.

On the Piste

maddogski.com

Freeride
T +33 (0)4 79 00 52 21
W freeride.fr
Route de la Montée, at the entrance of the Tremplin centre (above Jack's bar).
Wide choice of equipment alongside good accessories.

Boardbrains
T +33 (0)4 79 08 52 96
W boardbrains.com
Gallerie des Cimes, Route du Centre.
Boarding specialists offering a rental and sales service.

Online hire companies
freeride.fr
skihigher.com
skiset.com
sport2000.fr
twinner.org

Piste rankings

Pistes can sometimes be confusing – a red run can feel more 'black' than 'red' and vice versa, and for more experienced skiers looking for moguls or steeps, the piste ranking system is too broad to really be useful.

Mad Dog teamed up with New Generation (>33) ski school to rank the red and black pistes in the Three Valleys using a star system (* = easier and *** = more challenging).

Apart from gradient and width, there are other factors to consider:

- North or south: north-facing slopes are more inclined to be icy, but keep snow longer
- Traffic: less busy pistes can keep their snow longer but may not be pisted as often
- Grooming: the easier blues and greens tend to be pisted more frequently than the reds and blacks: some pistes are never groomed at all
- Weather: has there been recent snow? Is it windy?

The piste rankings
- Pistes are listed in alphabetical order by valley: reds first, then blacks
- Connecting lifts are in CAPITALS

Ski kit

Good kit is essential to keep you safe on the slopes. If you have any worries about your equipment, go back to the shop to ask for advice or exchange what you have.

Ski boots

Ski boots can be awkward but they shouldn't be painful. When you try them, wear the socks you're going to ski in and keep your thermals and ski trousers out of the boot. Your feet should feel snug but make sure your toes don't touch the front of the boot when you are in the right skiing position – you should be able to wiggle them easily.

Short toenails are essential – otherwise they bang against the front of the boot.

Snowboard boots

Snowboard boots are easier to walk in and softer than ski boots. They should be tight but not blood stopping; your toes should just touch the end and your heels shouldn't lift too much. The harder, stiffer versions are best for off-piste.

Skis

Most skis are 'carving' skis and have a 'waist' so that if you put them on their side and track them in the snow they draw a curve. This helps you turn more easily (rotate or tilt your feet to create an edge) making it quicker to learn and improve.

These skis are generally shorter than non-carving skis though off-piste versions are longer and wider (to help you 'float' in the powder).

The binding of your skis has something called the 'DIN'

On the Piste

Ski kit

setting. This dictates how easily the binding releases your boots, helping to avoid knee injuries. Children, beginners and lighter adults will have a lower setting.

Snowboards

Snowboards come in all shapes and sizes to cater for everything from the park (more flexible boards) to off-piste (stiffer) to ski touring (splitboards). If you're a beginner, the rental shop will generally give you a standard shaped board with a normal bindings setup until you know what sort of riding you prefer.

Buy or rent?

The quality of rental equipment is usually pretty good and gives you the chance to try the latest skis. However, if you ski for more than a week or two a year, it's definitely worth investing in custom-fit boots.

If you're thinking of buying your own kit, then end of season sales can see discounts of up to 50%.

Clothing

To adapt as the weather changes, wear layers, carry a hat and an extra fleece in your rucksack, even on sunny days in case the weather closes in. If you feel the cold, thermal glove liners are essential.

Red pistes – Méribel

Pistes	Comments
Alouette **	Narrow and steep at the top. The top gets lots of sun which affects the snow in warmer weather. PLATTIÈRES 3, ALLAMANDS, GRANGES
Blaireau *	Lovely, always well-groomed and easier than some blues (including Faon alongside it). TOUGNÈTE, ST MARTIN 1 & 2
Bd. Challe **	Cut-through path. ROC DE TOUGNE 1 & 2, TEPPES
Bouvreuil **	First section – after the bottom of Côte Brune lift – can get slushy when it's warm. PLATTIÈRES 2
Buse **/***	Cut-through path but steep and narrow. CHERFERIE
Campagnol **	Easiest of the two Mont Vallon reds but steep drop off from the narrow path at the top. MONT VALLON
Cerf ***	Great run but steep; if you fall you may slide all the way down. BURGIN 1
Chamois *	Long wide run. You can easily cut through to Biche at most points, though there is little difference between them. SAULIRE, VIZELLE, SUISSES, MARMOTTES, BURGIN 2, GRAND ROSIERE, COMBE

maddogski.com

Red pistes – Méribel

Pistes	Comments
Combe Vallon ***	Fantastic long run down from Mont Vallon, always mogulled – often quite challenging. MONT VALLON
Coqs **	Cut-through between runs. Always pisted. COMBES
Dahu ***	*** because access is via the steepest part of **Combe Tougnète** (albeit this is one of the easiest blacks in the Three Valleys). One of the first runs to lose snow later in the season.
Ecureuil ***	Steeper than **Combe Tougnète** which offers a similar route – not always pisted. TOUGNÈTE
Fouine **	Lovely red, quite steep but always pisted – usually has great snow. Access from Martre.
Lac de la Chambre **	Long and varied. Can get busy. Two sections where you need to schuss but you can see them coming. CÔTE BRUNE, 3 VALLÉES, BOUQUETIN
Lagopède ***	Steep red – great pitch all the way down. ROC DE TOUGNE 1 & 1, TEPPES
Marcassin **	Steep but sustained pitch all the way down. SAULIRE, VIZELLE, SUISSES, MARMOTTES, BURGIN 2, GRAND ROSIERE, COMBE
Mauduit ***	Named after local skier, Georges Mauduit. It was re-classified from black after some chalets were built at the top of the village. Can be icy at the bottom where you reach the trees. Not always pisted. SAULIRE, VIZELLE, SUISSES, MARMOTTES, BURGIN 2, GRAND ROSIERE, COMBE

Red pistes – Méribel

Pistes	Comments
Mouflon **	Nice classic red. PLATTIÈRES 3, ALLAMANDS, GRANGES
Niverolle **/***	Warrants *** if icy. Starts gently but the bottom section is very steep. SAULIRE, VIZELLE, SUISSES, MARMOTTES, BURGIN 2, GRAND ROSIERE, COMBE
Renard ***/**	Top half (from Dent de Burgin) is ***; after it crosses Bd de la Loze it is usually ** but not always pisted. Check it out from the chairlift and take Geai if you don't like the look of it. DENT DE BURGIN
Venturon **	Fantastic run down in the Méribel – Mottaret valley. Can be a little steep at the top. CÔTE BRUNE, 3 VALLÉES, BOUQUETIN

maddogski.com

Black pistes – Méribel

Pistes	Comments
Bartavelle **	Excellent bumps off to one side. Warrants *** if not pisted. Access from **Lagopède**.
Bosses ***	Long run with brilliant moguls pretty much all the way down. It gets the sun in the morning. Never pisted so only go down if you are a serious bumps fan. It's quite a public place to fall as it runs alongside Plan de l'homme. PLAN DE L'HOMME, ARPASSON
Chevreuil **	Can get bumpy and icy but great when pisted. There is a section which goes off camber at the bottom; watch out for those pylons. Runs off **Lièvre**.
Combe Tougnète **/*	Steep but wide entrance which can get icy. After that it flattens out into a red-level piste. TOUGNÈTE
Face **	Usually pisted but narrow. Always soft in the morning as it gets early sun. OLYMPIC
Grand Rosière ***	Can get mega-icy – beware! It can also have great bumps. Access is halfway down **Niverolle**.
Sanglier **	Lovely run, wide and fun all the way down. If it is pisted it moves down to *. SAULIRE, VIZELLE, SUISSES, MARMOTTES, BURGIN 2, GRAND ROSIERE, COMBE
Tetras **	Varied, interesting run, including a wide bumps section. Snow can get worn in warm weather. Usually quiet. LOZE, DOU DE LANCHE, COL DE LA LOZE

Red pistes – Courchevel

Pistes	Comments
Bd Amoureux **	Runs into Le Praz. Regularly snow cannoned to keep it open. Fairly flat but can be icy. Continuation of **Brigues** and **Jean Blanc**.
Bel Air *	Always well groomed, a wide longish red with fairly even pitch all the way down. BEL AIR
Bouc Blanc **	Two entrances – the steeper one is higher up the piste. The second entrance avoids the very top pitch, which is quite exposed and can get icy and rocky. In good snow, this is a joy to ski – wide and open all the way down towards La Tania. LOZE, PLANTREY, BOUC BLANC
Brigues **/***	The gradient, camber and direction change all the way down. North-facing, it can get icy in windy, cold weather. Snow cannons keep it is open pretty much all season. Runs from the bottom of EPICEA and PLANTREY
Cave des Creux **	South-facing, the bottom pitch can get bare in warm weather. Often quiet. GRAVELLES
Chapelets **	Steep top pitch which can get icy and quite mogulled. Not always groomed. In good conditions, this is one of the most fun reds in Courchevel, with varying pitches all the way down. SIGNAL

maddogski.com

Red pistes – Courchevel

Pistes	Comments
Combe Pylônes ***	Steep all the way down, but you can avoid the top pitch by taking a path which re-joins the piste part way down, and also gives an escape route halfway down onto **Combe Saulire**. (Ski past the top of the piste to access the path). If you fall in icy conditions, be prepared to slide. VIZELLE, SUISSES, MARMOTTES, CREUX NOIRS
Combe Saulire **/***	Three entrances – the easiest is the path to the right of the central entrance as you stand at the top. The most challenging steep and narrower entrance is on the far left (only accessible from SAULIRE). Busy at the end of the day as people come back into the resort. VIZELLE, SUISSES, SAULIRE, MARMOTTES, CREUX NOIRS
Combe Roc Mugnier ***	Avoid the steepest top part by taking a path entrance to the right – although this is also quite challenging. In icy conditions you may feel like you are just linking slides unless you have really good edges. ROC MUGNIER
Creux *	Probably the easiest red in Courchevel. Long and wide with something for everyone – wide open spaces at the top, fabulous views, ski through the trees at the bottom. It can get busy. The bottom half is in the shade till late morning early in the season so the snow can change from top to bottom. VIZELLE, SUISSES, SAULIRE, MARMOTTES, CREUX NOIRS
Dou du midi ***	Long run from 1850 to 1550. Steep (but wide) part at the top which earns it *** – otherwise it is a great run where you can feel a sense of achievement at the bottom. LOZE, PLANTREY, BOUC BLANC

Red pistes – Courchevel

Pistes	Comments
Dev. 1550 *	Runs off **Brigues** and **Jean Blanc**.
Jean Pachod ***	Fantastic in good conditions but it's rare for it to be good all the way down. Quite variable terrain – steep, then a narrow path leads onto a wider section which can get small moguls or rocky. The sun is on this run late morning to afternoon. CHANROSSA, ROC MERLET
Lac Creux *	This is a path connecting two pistes. Runs off **Creux**.
Lanches ***	There's not a lot going for this access route to La Tania. Steep start, followed by a flat path and a wider part with an odd camber, before it joins **Bouc Blanc**. PRAZ JUGET, CRETES, COQS, CHENUS
Marmottes ***	The top pitch is probably more ** but lower down it can get steep and bumpy. It has been widened in recent years to make it easier. VIZELLE, SUISSES, MARMOTTES, CREUX NOIRS
Marquetty ***	Short but bumpy and hardly ever pisted. Can get icy. BIOLLAY
Mur ***	This means 'wall' in French, probably because of the two steep parts, punctuated by flatter sections. Facing south, it can suffer in warm weather. Not always pisted. Runs off Altiport.

Red pistes – Courchevel

Pistes	Comments
Murettes **/***	Beautiful run in good conditions – down through the trees to Le Praz. Two access points both similar in difficulty. In icy conditions this warrants a *** rating. Runs off **Jockeys** and **Moretta blanche**.
Park City **	Wide and steep. Great views towards 1650. AIGUILLE DE FRUIT
Petit Dou **	Classic red. Often quiet despite coming into the centre of 1850. LOZE, PLANTREY
Petit Lac **	Short run which doesn't get much sun. BIOLLAY, PRALONG
Rama ***	Similar to **Marmottes**. The bottom half can get messy at the end of the day. Runs off **Park City**.
Rochers * & ***	The top half is *, the steeper bottom half ***. Tends to be quiet. SIGNAL
Roches Grises ***	Steep and bumpy – great if that's your thing. CREUX NOIRS
Roc Merlet **	Very short red run. ROC MERLET, CHANROSSA

Black pistes – Courchevel

Pistes	Comments
Chanrossa **	Steep for the top two-thirds. Doesn't get too busy. The bottom third flattens out with rollers – keep your speed up. ROC MERLET, CHANROSSA
Couloir de Belges ***	Bumpy, narrow and unpisted at the top – watch out for rocks except in good snow. Widens out after the initial entrance. The snow can get hard. VIZELLE, SUISSES, MARMOTTES, CREUX NOIRS
Dou de Lanches	Originally a red piste, there are only two steep pitches on this run – you can avoid the second icier section by cutting through to **Bouc Blanc** on the right after the first steep section. Try not to fall on the lower section as it is right under the Dou de Lanches chair. DOU DE LANCHES
Grand Couloir ***+	This infamous black is allegedly the steepest in Europe – nearly 40 degrees at the top section. It's certainly one of the hardest in the Three Valleys. After the nerve-wracking narrow ridge – the only way in – you then have to deal with steep bumps, which can be lethal in icy conditions. It gets more crowded on Fridays as many people wait till the end of the week before they attempt it. SAULIRE
Jean Blanc **	Together with **Jockeys**, this is what blacks are all about; varied terrain, steep sections, tree-lined (so usually excellent for low visibility conditions). Part way down, you can get onto **Brigues** to Le Praz or **Deviation** to reach 1550. PLANTREY, BOUC BLANC, LOZE

maddogski.com

Black pistes – Courchevel

Pistes	Comments
Jockeys **	Jockeys leads off **Bouc Blanc** just above the La Tania gondola. **> Jean Blanc**. PLANTREY, LOZE, BOUC BLANC
M **	The last pitch can get icy. VIZELLE, SUISSES, MARMOTTES, CREUX NOIRS
Suisses *	Lots of different entrance options – if you come in under the chair, you will be taking *** route with a more gentle entrance from **Marmottes** or the top of AIGUILLE DE FRUIT. VIZELLE, SUISSES, MARMOTTES, CREUX NOIRS
Turcs *	Short run linking pistes. VIZELLE, SUISSES, MARMOTTES, CREUX NOIRS

Red pistes – Les Menuires and St Martin

Pistes	Comments
4 Vents *	Lovely run, though there's a steep section towards the bottom. Access from **Bd de la lance** and Mont de la Chambre.
Allamands *	Cruisy red all the way to Les Menuires. One or two steep parts but they are always on wide sections. ALLAMANDS, PLATTIÈRES 3
Becca **	Nice run. BECCA
Bd de la lance *	Link piste.
Combes ***	Can be icy and also is one of the first slopes to get worn in less perfect conditions. Access from Liason and **David Douillet Haut**.
Crêtes **	MASSE 2
David *** Douillet Haut & Bas	Gets icy, bumpy and busy. As a consequence, can be one of the first to get worn if it hasn't snowed for a while. The piste is named after a gold medal judo champion who skis here with his family. MONT DE LA CHAMBRE, BRUYERES 2, CÔTE BRUNE
Fred Covili **	Fred Covili is a Grand Slalom world champion who hails from Les Menuires. This run is a classic red; usually it has great snow. MASSE 2

maddogski.com

Red pistes – Les Menuires and St Martin

Pistes	Comments
Jérusalem *	Long cruisy red which is often cited as a favourite. It can be stony after the narrow section between two rocks part way down. The bottom is not cannoned so snow texture can be quite different. Keep your speed up at the bottom. ST MARTIN 2, CHERFERIE, TOUGNÈTE
Les enverses **/*	Nice long run which is a little steeper towards the bottom. Runs from bottom of MASSE
Liason *	Cut-through path between pistes, but can be narrow and icy in places. Access from Lac des Combes from the top of BECCA
Montaulever *	The last pitch gets very busy which can create moguls. It also gets the sun so will have softer snow in warmer weather. BRUYERES 1
Pramint *	Another classic red run with a few fun rollers towards the bottom. You can cut out part way down into Pelozet which rejoins at the bottom of the piste. ST MARTIN 2, TOUGNÈTE
Rochers *	MASSE
Teppes *	TEPPES, ROC DE TOUGNE 1 & 2

Black pistes – Les Menuires and St Martin

Pistes	Comments
3 Marches **	Not often skied as you just end up back at the same chair. Icy first thing. ALLAMANDS, PLATTIÈRES 3
Aiglon **	Quite short, but often stony and exposed to the wind. ETÉLÉ
Dame blanche ***	One of the hardest blacks in the Three Valleys; mostly icy and very steep and can be bumpy too. MASSE
Etélé ***	Can be very bumpy, never groomed. ETÉLÉ
Lac Noir **	Runs on from **Crêtes** from the top of MASSE 2
Léo Lacroix **/***	Top section is steepest and most challenging. Runs off **Bd de la lance** and **David Douillet Haut**.
Masse **	Short, steep section at the top. MASSE 2
Pylônes ***	Never groomed, gets mogulled. MONT DE LA CHAMBRE
Rocher Noir **	Nice run. ROCHER NOIR

Red pistes – Val Thorens

Pistes	Comments
Béranger ***	There are four red options from the top of the Funitel Peclet; **Béranger** is the most difficult followed by **Lac Blanc**, then **Christine** then **Tête Ronde**. Each pair tends to be pisted on alternate days. As you go up in the Funitel, check which one has not been pisted. **Béranger** has a cut-through path on the left which is flatter but not always pisted. GLACIER, FUNITEL PECLET
Bd Cumin *	It's unclear why this is a red. Short steepish bit at the start but then a lovely flattish path run through the valley to Les Menuires. You may want to take it more slowly if you don't like narrow pistes. Not so easy for novice boarders. From the bottom of BOISMINT
Boismint **	BOISMINT
Bouchet **	Highest point in the four valleys and an access point for the Bouchet Glacier off-piste itinerary. BOUCHET
Chamois ***	Should be black but probably graded red as it's the only route back to the Val Thorens valley from Rosaël. It's not for the faint-hearted and in less perfect conditions it's not unusual to see people crying. There's a narrow path if you want to avoid the steep top pitch. FUNITEL, GRAND FOND, ROSAËL
Christine */**	See **Béranger**. GLACIER, FUNITEL PECLET

Red pistes – Val Thorens

Pistes	Comments
Col **	Keep your speed up off the chairlift to get to the top of the piste. Extremely dangerous to go off-piste here as it's surrounded by a glacier. There may be mogul on the top section. COL
Col de l'audzin ***	Great run with a 900m vertical drop. Because it's long, less experienced skiers may want to take it easy. Check out conditions from the cable car or on the daily piste map. CIME CARON
Falaise **	It can be easy to miss the access from **Chamois**.
Glacier **/***	North-facing slope, usually not busy so often has some of the best snow in the valley. *** rating is due to the steepness. GLACIER
Haute Combe **/***	South-facing piste so the condition depends mainly on the weather. BOISMINT
Lac blanc **	See **Béranger**. Steep section in the middle. FUNITEL PECLET, GLACIER
Mauriennaise **	South-facing, so the condition is variable. Escape route onto a blue towards the bottom of the piste. ROSAËL
Médaille *	Lovely run. FUNITEL GRAND FOND
Névés */**	Cut through between pistes. Access from Combe de Caron.

Red pistes – Val Thorens

Pistes	Comments
Plan de l'eau ***	Long steep section in the middle. PLAN DE L'EAU
Portette **/***	Sometimes icy. Under the lift can get bumpy. PORTETTE
Rhodos **/***	Quite often unpisted. Follows on from **Médaille**.
Tête ronde *	See **Béranger**. FUNITEL PECLET, GLACIER
Variante **/***	If it's windy at the top, the first pitch can be icy. FUNITEL GRAND FOND

Black pistes – Val Thorens

Pistes	Comments
Arolle **	Great bumps run – not pisted. MOUTIERE
Cascades ***	Great bumps run – not pisted. CASCADES
Combe de Caron **/***	Absolute must – a great black with fabulous views and a long run down the mountain. Can get bumps in places and a few steeper sections. CIME CARON
Combe Rosaël **/***	Its south-facing position makes the snow more variable. The bumps which build up on this run can get slushy in warm weather. CIME CARON
Marielle Goitschel */**	Two entrances – the right-hand one (go along the flat section at the top) is easier. Can get bumpy on the left. 3 VALLÉES, CÔTE BRUNE

Day trips

There are lots of great routes through the Three Valleys. Below are two of our favourites – download more at **maddogski.com:**
- St Martin, Mottaret and Mont Vallon
- The Courchevel valley
- The fourth valley

The Three Valleys escapade

This challenge, designed by the tourist office as a great way to discover the Three Valleys, reaches the furthest points of the ski domain including the top of the glaciers in Orelle and Val Thorens. Pick up a plan and route map from the lift office or tourist office.

For good skiers who know the area, with a little planning the escapade can be done in one day, or you can cover it at a more leisurely pace over a few days. Follow the symbols on the piste map (yellow arrows on a small green circle) collecting a stamp at each of the 14 checkpoints – they're all different so you can't cheat. If you're planning to do this in one day, make sure you take sandwiches to eat on the go. On completion, you can proudly collect your certificate at the lift office and also buy an 'exclusive' medal for €7.

About the day trips

Aim to start these trips around 9am, avoiding the ski school queues that start to build up from 9.30am at the main lifts (schools have priority queuing). Timings are based on the pace of a competent red-run skier and assume good conditions and average lift queues. Allow additional time if you are skiing more slowly or during school holidays when lifts can have longer waiting times. If you're leaving the Méribel valley, it's better to be less ambitious than to miss the last connecting lift home, which can result in a very expensive taxi fare.

All piste directions assume you are facing downhill, although lift directions refer to the way you are facing as you get off.

Our researchers have worked hard to make these itineraries as accurate as possible. However, pistes and routes can change from season to season so please take a piste map with you in case anything is unclear.

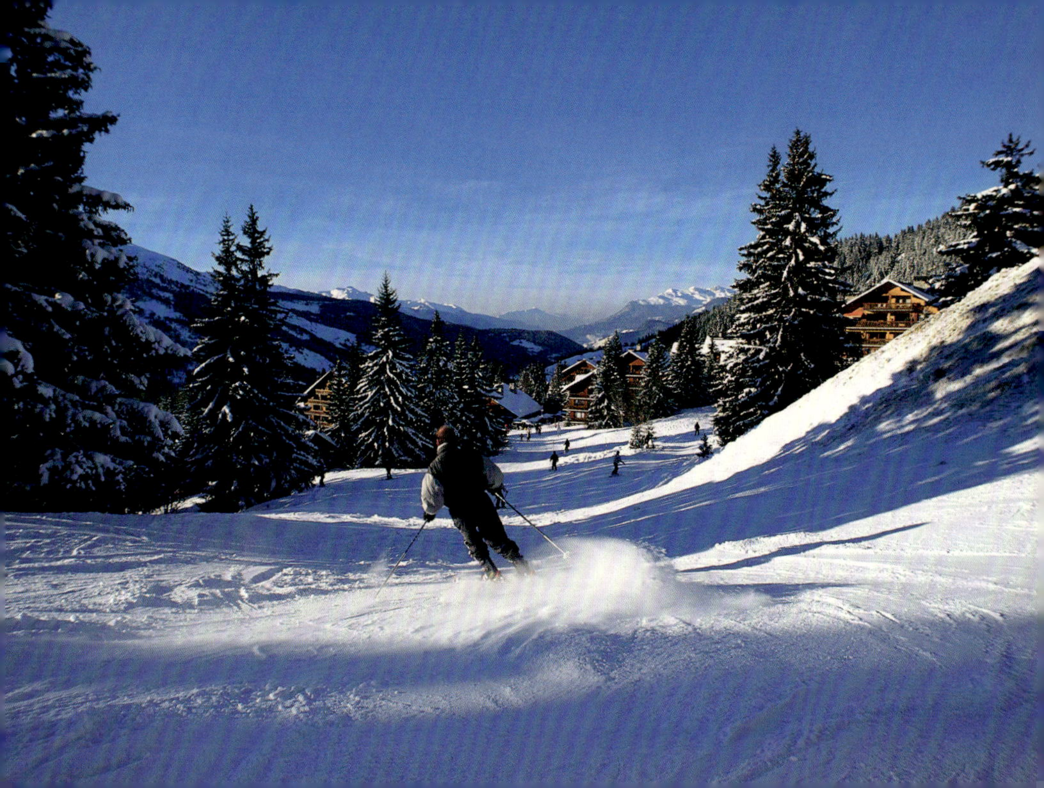

The Méribel villages

This tour takes you the length of the Méribel valley from Mottaret to Le Raffort or Les Allues (as long as snow conditions allow) with a brief ski over into Les Menuires valley. This is a gentle day ideal for getting your ski-legs back. It has some long blues and pretty tree-lined runs.

If you feel like a shorter day, it is relatively easy to head back home at almost any point.

Lifts	Comments
Plan de L'homme	Turn left at the top and follow **Grives** as far as the Tougnète gondola mid-station. From there ski below and then to the right of the gondola and follow **Perdrix** until you reach Mottaret village (after a flattish section running alongside some large buildings). Head for the gondola on your right as you ski into the village.
Pas du Lac 1 & 2	Get off at the second stop. Ski right out of the lift building and once you reach the ridge between Courchevel and Méribel, follow signs for Mottaret. Take **Niverolle** which runs into **Aigle** around the mid-station area. Keep going till you reach Mottaret village once more; this time take the gondola on your left as you reach the village.
Plattières 1,2 & 3	Stop for a break at the top.

Lifts	Comments
Break	**Le Roc des 3 Marches (> 102).** Self-service with great views on three sides of the terrace. From here take Grand Lac and then Pelozet towards St Martin. When you reach the point where the two St Martin lifts meet take the chairlift.
St Martin 2	Turn left at the top following Crêtes and Choucas back into the Méribel valley. Choucas runs into Escargot and just past the bottom of the Olympic chair take a left onto Villages. This is a great run through the trees but does depend on good snow conditions. Take the side turning to Le Raffort – this is a better run than continuing down to Les Allues (unless the snow is really good). Note: If Villages is shut through lack of snow, continue on to Gelinotte to Méribel and pick up the itinerary after the next lift.
Olympe 3	This takes you to just near the Chaudanne in Méribel. You will need to walk a short distance to the next lift.
Rhodos 1	On your left as you head into the Chaudanne lift area. Get off at the first stop and ski down and to the right where you will see Le Rond Point on your right next to the road.
Lunch	**Le Rond Point (> 95).** Lively restaurant and bar with food to suit all budgets. From here ski back to the Chaudanne and takes Rhodos again.

Lifts	Comments
Rhodos 1 & 2	This time get off at the second stop and join **Blanchot** following it down past the bottom of the Altiport lift. Keep your speed up here and ski over the small bridge and follow the lovely tree-lined **Lapin** all the way down to Méribel-Village
Golf	Ski straight off this lift onto Altiport
Altiport	Turn right and ski back under the lift stopping at Dent de Burgin part way down **Blanchot**.
Dent de Burgin	Take **Renard** back down to the bottom of the same lift – there are often some good moguls off to the side of this piste.
Dent de Burgin	Turn right and ski a short distance to take **Geai** turning left just before the Rhodos gondola joining **Rhodos**, **Doron**.
Finish	**Make the cosy Adray Télébar (see mountain restaurants) your last stop of the day.** Pedestrians can also meet you here (although they will have a short walk across the piste). Afterwards it is a short ski back to the Chaudanne.

St Martin, Mottaret and Mont Vallon

This itinerary takes you up to the Tougnète ridge, making the most of the morning sun on those slopes. Your mid-morning break is in St Martin and instead of lunch on the mountain you drop down into Mottaret (still with great views of the slopes) and have lunch at Au Temps Perdu. After lunch you take in the fabulous Mont Vallon area at the furthest end of the Méribel valley before heading home.

Lifts	Comments
Plan de L'Homme	Take this chairlift out of the Chaudanne. Turn right at the top and take Escargot a short distance until you reach the Cherferie drag lift on your left. You'll need to keep your speed up to ski across to the bottom of the lift.
Cherferie	A longish drag. At the top, turn right and follow signs for St Martin, taking the turn off for the lovely Jérusalem. Keep your speed up as it flattens out toward the end and you head left to join Verdet. This brings you out near two restaurants and the St Martin 2 chairlift. Ski past the closest restaurant and turn right onto Biolley leading to St Martin village. As you reach the bottom, ski under the small bridge, bear left and head for the St Martin gondala.
St Martin 1	Walk to the restaurant next door to the top station of this left.
Break	**Take a break in Le Chardon Bleu (> 99), making the most of the deck chairs and sunny terrace.** After you stop, cross the piste and take the chairlift.

Lifts	Comments
St Martin 2	Turn right off the top and then immediately right on **Pramint**. This is a great 'ego' red – wide but with enough steep sections to feel challenging. You join up with **Pelozet** to reach the same chairlift again.
St Martin 2	Turn right at the top following a ridge and signs for **Gros Tougne** which you follow until you reach two lifts. Take the covered chairlift.
Granges	Follow **Mouflon** taking you back into the Méribel valley. This joins up with two blues, **Sittelle** and **Rossignol**. You can take either – both join **Martre** and you end up in Mottaret village.
Lunch	**Au Temps Perdu (> 76).** Walk towards the shops with Olympic Ski and Le Grenier restaurant on your right. Au Temps Perdu is tucking in amongst the shops. It has an outside terrace with views of the pistes. They serve a range of salads, crêpes and pasta dishes (as well as good choice for vegetarians). Service is always friendly and efficient. If you want something quicker or lighter, try the snack bar Le Chrismaran under Le Grenier restaurant. After lunch take Plattières.
Plattières	There are three stops on the Plattières lift. You should get off at the second. Ski left back under the gondala taking either **Bouvreuil** or **Bouvreuil** to Mont Vallon.

Lifts	Comments
Mont Vallon	Wide views at the top and two lovely red runs with views down the valley. **Campagnol** is the easier of the two. When you have skied one, take the lift back up and ski the other. With **Combe Vallon** you'll need to take the Mures Rouges chair to bring you back to Mont Vallon. Once you have finished playing around Mont Vallon take Plan des Mains chairlift (near to the Mont Vallon gondola). Note: Don't be tempted to take Ours; it's incredibly flat and you'll almost certainly end up walking.
Plan des Mains	Turns right of the top and follow **Rossignol** or **Sittelle**. Both join up with **Martre** and take you back to Mottaret.
Finish	**Have your last stop on the terrace of the Côte Brune restaurant.** Afterwards take **Truite** to Méribel. The start of this piste is just to the right of where you had lunch – next to the large wooden mountain-shaped building you'll see as you look down the valley.

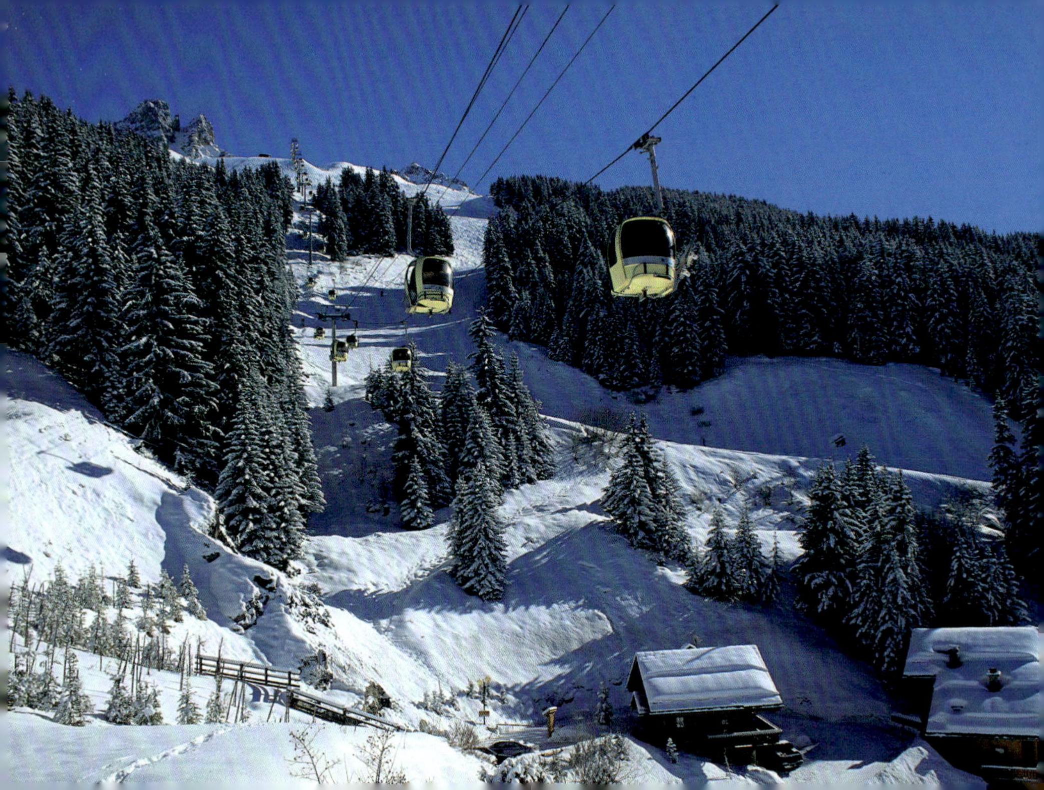

Where to find the best **food and drink** in resort and on the mountain, from regional specialities to luxurious restaurants.

What you'll find in this chapter

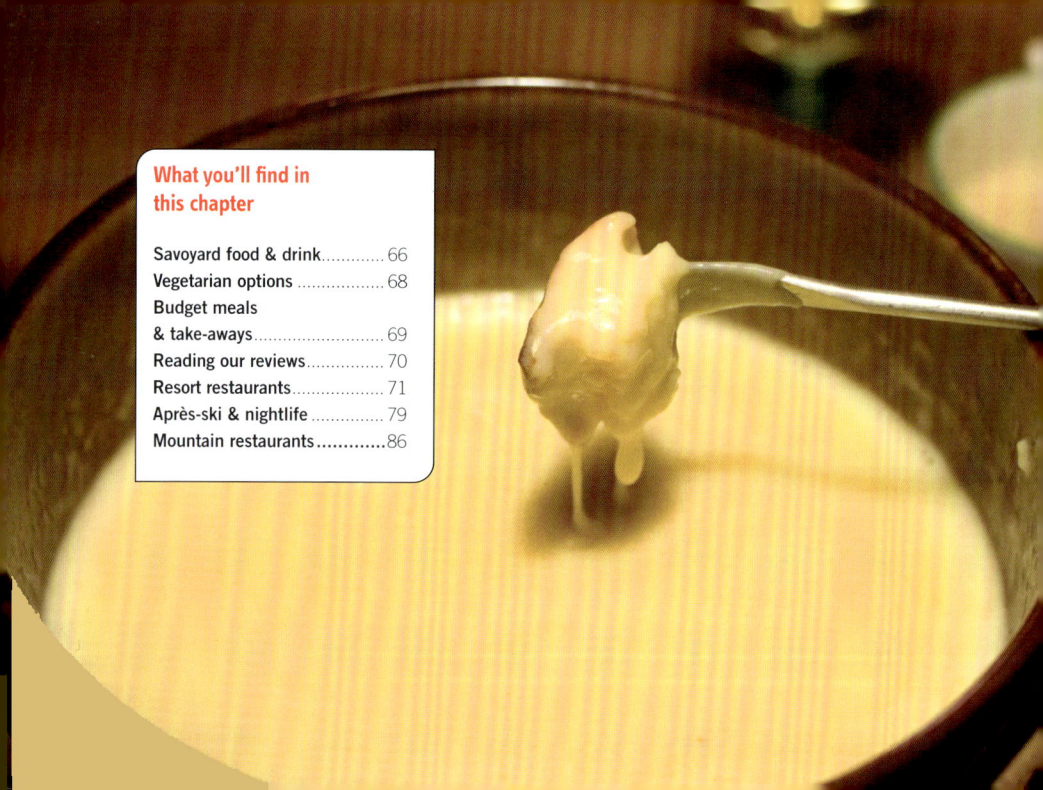

Savoyard food & drink	66
Vegetarian options	68
Budget meals & take-aways	69
Reading our reviews	70
Resort restaurants	71
Après-ski & nightlife	79
Mountain restaurants	86

Méribel may not have the Michelin-starred restaurants of nearby Courchevel, but it does have huge variety of places to eat and the prices tend to be more affordable.

Special diets

I am vegetarian
Je suis vegetarien(ne)
…but I can eat fish
mais je peux manger des poissons
I cannot eat nuts/dairy products/wheat
Je ne peux pas manger des noix/des produits laitiers/du blé

The *'plat du jour'* (dish of the day) and fixed price menus are usually good value, particularly in mountain restaurants. The menu is usually a two-course option (starter plus main course or main course plus dessert) but some restaurants also offer gastronomic tasting menus.

Finally, don't feel you have to eat and drink just in the village you are staying in. There is a free bus service and it is well worth exploring what the rest of the resort has to offer.

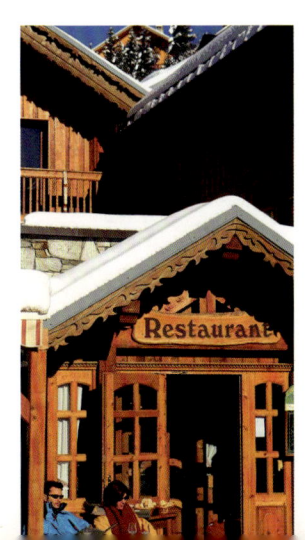

Food and drink

What's at steak?

Carnivores have a treat in store. Fantastic steaks are available at reasonable prices in many establishments – our favourites are **Chez Kiki** (➤ 73) and **Les Enfants Terribles** (➤ 74).

Blue	*bleu*
Rare	*saignant (pronounced 'sanyon')*
Medium	*à point*
Well done	*bien cuit*
Steak tartare	raw minced beef mixed with onions, herbs and spices
Pavé	thick cut rump steak
Entrecôte	similar to rib eye – fatty but flavoursome
Faux-filet	similar to sirloin
Filet	similar to fillet steak
Côte de boeuf	a huge side of beef normally served on the bone with sauces. Perfect for sharing

Show some respect

Hundreds of glaciers have melted in the last 150 years.

Join our Respect the Mountain campaign to save those still standing.

Buy a green wristband and visit **respectthemountain.com** to discover how you can make a difference.

respectthemountain.com

Mad Dog Ski supports respectthemountain.com

Savoyard food

Beaufort	a hard cheese made from the milk of the local mahogany-coloured Beaufort cows.
Chevrotin	a soft, almost sweet goats cheese that is perfect after a meal with some wine or port.
Crozets	tiny squares of pasta that are traditionally served in a sauce of local cheese, ham and cream.
Diots	local sausages – usually quite a strong flavour – in plain, cheese or cabbage variations. Definitely an acquired taste.
Fondue	either a bubbling cauldron of oil that you cook chunks of meat in or else a mix of cheeses and spirits to dip bread into. Normally ordered for two or more.
Raclette	a grill with a large lump of cheese is brought to your table. As the cheese melts, scrape it onto cold meats, potatoes and salad. Normally ordered for two or more.
Reblochon	a local cheese that has a delicious flavour and an easily recognisable pungent aroma – you'll smell it in all Savoyard restaurants. Originally made with the milk from the second milking (the 'rebloche').
Pierre chaude	a hot stone on which you cook a variety of meats on your table. Sprinkle the stone with salt before cooking to prevent sticking.
Tartiflette	an extremely satisfying mix of potato, bacon, cream and reblochon cheese which is then baked in the oven. A variation – Tartichèvre is made with goat's cheese.
Tomme de Savoie	an ivory-coloured, delicate cheese often made with skimmed milk and therefore lower in fat.

Savoyard drink

Chartreuse	loopy juice in the shape of a spirit – nice when added to hot chocolate (green chaud).
Demi beer	beer is generally drunk in halves in France. Sometimes served with peach syrup (demi pêche), which is much nicer than it sounds. A larger beer is called 'un serieux'. Ask for a 'pression' if you would like draft lager.
Eau de vie	a digestif (so called because it is supposed to aid digestion). Good ones are delicious but bad ones can be akin to petrol.
Génépi	famous for its local digestive values (when taken in moderation), this local tipple is made from the Genepi flower. Picking is strictly controlled and, if you're offered a homemade bottle of the stuff, it's so delicious you can see why.
Kir	an aperitif glass of white wine with a fruit liqueur added – usually cassis (blackcurrant), mure (blackberry) or framboise (raspberry).
Mutzig	super strong beer and very tasty.
Vin chaud	hot mulled wine.

Food and drink

maddogski.com

Vegetarian options

If you're vegetarian, as always in France finding options other than pizza, pasta or cheese fondue is not easy, though definitely not impossible. Many restaurants don't seem to understand the concept of vegetarian food, although we've found a few with a decent vegetarian menu. With catered chalet holidays, you can usually be confident that you'll at least get some variety throughout the week.

Children

Children are welcome in all restaurants and most places will have a kid's menu or half portions on offer. Our favourite family-friendly restaurants are listed in **Children** (> 123).

French wine

The Savoie has been producing local wine for at least 900 years, but unless you've visited the region, you're unlikely to have tried it.

So, what to expect? The most popular wines are Apremont, Chignan and Gamay. Gamay (a grape variety) is often used to make Savoie reds. It's also the grape used in the better-known Beaujolais region. It makes light fruity reds that can be drunk very young, but generally don't keep for long.

Apremont and Chignan are villages close to Chambéry, where the Jacquere grape is the most used. These wines are light and crisp and often seem slightly fizzy. As a rule, if you order a local white wine in resort, they will serve Apremont.

The Altesse grape makes a full bodied white, resonant of unoaked Chardonnay and usually labelled Rousette de Savoie. If you prefer reds, try Mondeuse – the original Savoie red grape. It is full bodied and spicy (although you'll never find an Aussie Shiraz equivalent here as the climate is very different).

Which wine with which food?

A general rule in France is that regional wines go well with the traditional food of the region. However, this rule is harder to follow here – mainly because the traditional Savoyard dishes are so firmly based around cheese. In spite of all those wonderful cheese and wine parties people hold, cheese is one of the things that really spoils wine because it coats your mouth, thus rendering you unable to appreciate the finer intricacies of the drink.

Our advice with Savoyard cooking would be to drink whatever you fancy. The lighter whites such as Apremont and Chignan are best as an aperitif, although they are acidic enough to cut through oilier fish flavours. Gamay is a good choice for white meat with sauces, fish and lighter red meats. In fact, served slightly chilled, it's very refreshing in the summer. Choose a Mondeuse for red meat.

But don't just take our word for it, get out there are try them. As a rule, these wines don't travel well so are best drunk locally.

Budget meals and take-aways

You can usually tell by the appearance of a restaurant whether it will break the bank or not. Most of the pizza restaurants and British bars offer cheaper meals.

If you fancy a night in, then **Le Refuge** (> 75), **Pizza 32** in Mussillon next to the Spar and **Pizza Express** (> 75) all do take-aways.

For lunch on the go, there are a number of designated picnic areas with tables and chairs throughout the Three Valleys (you'll see them marked on your piste map) – or you can just improvise by sitting on upturned skis or boards. > 118 for food shops.

For something a bit special, **Picnics on the Piste** (picnicsonthepiste.co.uk) will deliver a picnic to you on the mountain. Choose from four different menus ranging from the green picnic of baguettes, cheeses and meats to the black picnic of foie gras, smoked salmon and chocolates.

How to read our reviews

Resort restaurants (➤73) and bars (➤79) are listed in alphabetical order. Mountain restaurants (➤86) are alphabetical by valley.

- 🪙 budget: most main courses are under €10
- 🪙🪙 mid-range: most main courses range from €10-20
- 🪙🪙🪙 expensive: most main courses are over €20
- V good vegetarian choice
- LATE venues that stay open late (1am or after)
- 🐕 our absolute **Mad Dog** favourites

Resort restaurants

The high number of chalets in Méribel can make it difficult to get a table on the staff night off (usually Wednesday or Thursday). Restaurants often have two sittings and it's best to make your reservation as soon as possible to get the time that suits you.

Our absolute favourites... and why

These are places that our researchers return to time and time again:

Adray Télébar > 93	Wonderful mountain hideaway that also serves supper
Chez From'ton > 73	The best fondue in town
Chez Kiki > 73	Welcoming restaurant above the village
Le Cro Magnon > 73	Good French cooking in a cosy local setting
Evolution > 74	Relaxed modern restaurant near the Chaudanne
Le Refuge > 75	Lovely thin pizzas to eat in or take-away
La Tsaretta > 85	Consistently good food in the pretty village of Les Allues

Food and drink

maddogski.com

Méribel bars and restaurants

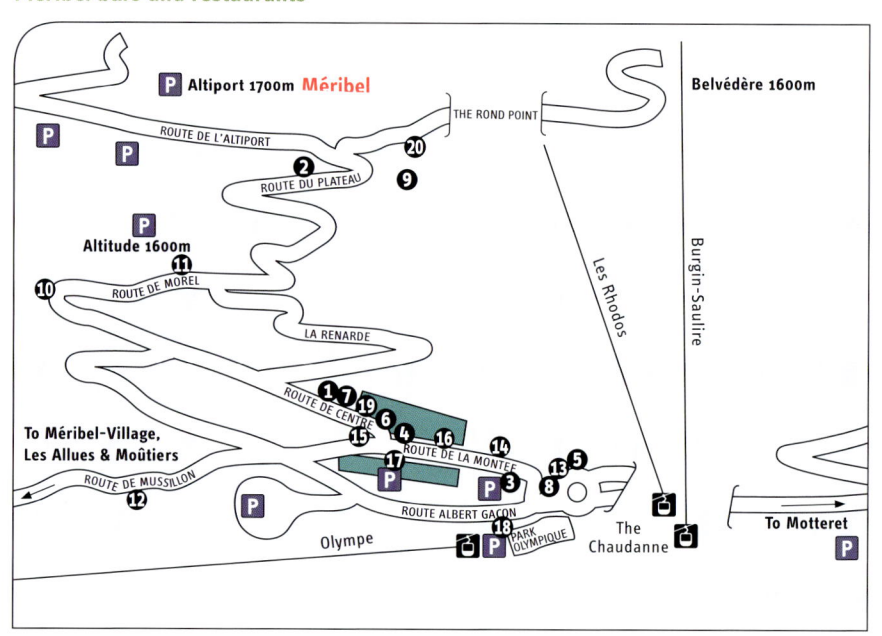

Key:

1. Chez From'ton
2. Le Cro Magnon
3. La Flambée
4. Le Refuge
5. Cactus Café
6. Scott's Bar and le Pub
7. La Galette
8. Evolution
9. Adray Télébar
10. Chez Kiki
11. Les Enfants Terribles
12. Pizza Express and Dicks Tea Bar
13. Le Tremplin
14. Grand Marnier Crêpes
15. La Taverne
16. Fifty50
17. Barometre
18. Le Loft
19. Le Poste
20. Le Rond Point

Méribel

Chez From'ton

T +33 (0)4 79 08 55 48

Route du Centre in the Galerie des Cimes, downstairs from the La Fromagerie cheese shop, 7-9.30pm.
Cosy restaurant specialising in cheese – the perfect place for a fondue (the house version is particularly good).

Chez Kiki

T +33 (0)4 79 08 66 68

Route de Morel, 7-11.30pm.
Big meals – a lot of meat, including wonderful steak – are cooked over the open fire in this welcoming place. A little outside the main hub of the resort, it's well worth the short walk/bus ride up the hill (towards the Rond-Point).

Le Cro Magnon

T +33 (0)4 79 00 57 38

Plateau de Morel, near the Rond Point. Access from Méribel is on the 'Altiport' or 'Belvédère' buses or a short taxi ride, 7-11.30pm.
You can spot this restaurant by the large model of an early homo sapien outside. Inside it's a small, typically French restaurant which is popular with locals and families. Thoughtful service and a menu that includes pizza, fondue and brochette. A

maddogski.com

particularly good choice if you're staying near the Rond Point as it's just a short walk down the road from there, in the direction of Méribel.

Les Enfants Terribles
T +33 (0)4 79 08 64 62

Route de Morel (Méribel 1600), 4pm-1am (food served 7-10pm).
This is definitely somewhere to head if you're staying in the satellite area between Méribel and the Rond-Point. The open fire and candlelight make it cosy and the staff are welcoming. Reliable cooking served in a busy but friendly atmosphere – make sure you book.

Evolution
T +33 (0)4 79 00 44 26

Near the Chaudanne, 8am-10.30pm.
Evolution is a lively place where there always seems to be something going on. Food is tasty and varied (wild mushroom risotto and chicken stuffed with goat's cheese, for example). There's a skiers' lunch menu, served with the promise that if you don't get your lunch in 20 minutes you don't pay. Well worth a visit.

La Flambée
T +33 04 79 00 31 70

Route de la Montée, near the Chaudanne, 12-2.30pm, 7-10pm.
Bubbly Italian restaurant, complete with murals on the walls. A good place for a relaxed supper. Pizzas and spectacular-looking calzones are cooked in the wood-fired oven. Aubergine lasagne is filling but not too heavy and a welcome change for vegetarians. Other options include saltimbocca and fillet steak.

La Galette
T +33 (0)4 79 08 53 90

In the Galerie des Cimes, Route du Centre, 12pm-midnight.
Great cosy atmosphere inside and out, with an accessible menu of galettes, pizza, fondue and raclette.

Great for families (try the kir Breton made with local cider). The full menu is served all day.

Grand Marnier Crêpes

Route de la Montée, a short walk from the Chaudanne (on the right as you head to the main square).
Lovely crêpes freshly made in front of you with a choice of every filling you can imagine. A handy snack-stop on your way home at the end of the day.

Pizza Express

T +33 (0)4 79 08 98 58

Route de Mussillon, next to Dicks Tea Bar (10 minute walk from the main square in the direction of Méribel Village), 5.50pm-1am.
No need to explain this one – it has the same menu and décor as at home. The only difference is that it's also a bar and has live music some nights. A handy place to eat (early) if you have kids or (late) if you're planning a night out at Dicks Tea Bar. Entrance is free if you eat here. If you're driving, there's a car park opposite.

Le Refuge

T +33 (0)4 79 08 61 97
Route de la Montée (tourist office end), 12-2.30pm, 7-10pm (closed Sundays).
The dark wood and simple red décor make this family-run restaurant feel immediately welcoming. Downstairs is informal with good, simple food including salmon pasta and roast chicken. The pizzas (thin and perfect) are also available to take-away. The upstairs restaurant opens in the evenings – it is more fancy and prices rise accordingly, but it's a good choice if you want to linger over supper.

Scott's Bar
T +33 (0)4 79 00 39 61

🪙

Main square, 4pm-1.30am (bar food served 5-10pm).
Near the tourist office. American-style snacks to line your stomach – nachos, pizzas or the mighty combo selection for two. > 84.

La Taverne
T +33 (0)4 79 00 36 18

🪙

Opposite the tourist office, 7.30am-1am, MC €6-11, HW €9.
This place has all bases covered. Hotel Le Roc is upstairs (> 16), the bar provides entertainment by way of pool, table football and live music and the internet café has high-speed terminals. There's a small terrace which is perfect for (good) early morning coffee and in the evening more elaborate food is served in the popular basement restaurant. In between (from mid-morning) you can buy snacks such as hamburgers and sandwiches. Generous happy hours. The bar itself is simple and wooden – a relaxed après-ski scene but can get crowded as the night wears on. Popular with seasonaires.

Brasserie Le Tremplin
T +33 (0)4 79 00 37 95

🪙

The Chaudanne, opposite the Parc Olympique, 8am-10pm.
A relaxed, family-friendly place convenient for the slopes with a lovely large terrace. The food is reliable and the menu ranges from pizzas to oysters. Mid-priced meals include tartiflette and steak and chips. Staff never rush you, even when it's busy, and are always welcoming. Children's menu available.

Mottaret
Au Temps Perdu
T +33 (0)4 79 00 36 64

🪙

In the main piste area near the shopping centre, 12-10pm.
Brisk service, smiley staff and a sunny terrace make this a pleasant lunch-stop. There are various salads including Roquefort

Mad Dog Ski Méribel

and walnut, pastas (from €12) and crêpes (from €9). The more elaborate evening menu, which includes Savoyard specialities, is served in the restaurant's cellar.

Le Grenier
T +33 (0)4 79 00 44 33

In the main piste area, 12-3pm, 6-11pm.
An unusual little place. At lunchtime you are peacefully suspended above the hubbub of the piste below and can watch people skiing down into Mottaret. There is quite a meat-based menu, including beef fillet and duck breast with honey, but you'll also find plenty of Savoyard specialities.

Pizzeria du Mottaret
T +33 (0)4 79 00 40 50

In the main piste area (next to the pharmacy), 11am-10pm.
Jolly pizzeria with a small terrace at the front. They also serve Savoyard dishes and steak.

Méribel-Village
Lodge du Village
T +33 (0)4 79 01 03 55

Centre of the village (ski access is by Lapin), 11am-1am (food served 12-4.30pm, 7-10pm).
LDV is something of an institution in Méribel-Village – no doubt you will come across it in one of its guises, be it bar, restaurant or live-music venue. The breezy yellow ground-floor restaurant has a predominantly Italian menu which includes crostini, pizza and chicken with ham and gorgonzola. The restaurant has clearly made an effort not to overlook vegetarians and there are always a few options for them to choose from. When it's sunny, lunch is served on the terrace.

Les Allues
La Croix Jean-Claude
T +33 (0)4 79 08 61 05

Place du Four, 12-2pm, 7-10pm.
Just past the town hall, this hotel has a reputation for reliable regional

maddogski.com

cooking and its old-world calm makes a welcome change from the English buzz higher up the mountain. There are Savoyard specialities such as fondue as well as foie gras and lamb. Late in the season, when the snow on the lower slopes starts to melt, they serve wild salad leaves picked from the mountain. There is also a quiet little bar frequented by locals.

La Tsaretta
T +33 (0)4 79 08 61 00

Route des Carons, opposite the church – take the second right past the Hotel La Croix Jean-Claude, 5pm-1.30am every day (upstairs restaurant serves food from 7-10pm).

Another of the 'three in one' places that Méribel does so well; the friendly English staff run a busy bar downstairs, there's regular live music till late and upstairs is a restaurant set in the wooden eaves overlooking the village's enchanting church. The menu has been thoughtfully put together to include good choices for vegetarians and meat eaters, including food you don't often see on the mountain such as spare ribs and Thai prawn curry. Don't overlook this one just because you aren't staying in Les Allues.

Après-ski & nightlife

When the lifts close, there's something to suit every taste and budget in Méribel. Given its reputation for hosting groups of English, some people shrink from the resort's nightlife – but don't. Although the English presence is strong in some places there's plenty of alternative venues. You can stop off at cosy mountain lodges for a final vin chaud before the last run home, enjoy a beer in tiny one-bar bars away from the piste or listen to a live band.

Most bars are quiet during the dinner period of 6.30-9.30pm and will not get going again until after 10pm. This may seem late but it's surprising how energetic you can feel after a couple of glasses of wine.

How to read our reviews

Resort restaurants (>73) and bars (>79) are listed in alphabetical order. Mountain restaurants (>86) are alphabetical by valley.

- budget: a small beer is around €3
- mid-range: a small beer is around €3-5
- expensive: a small beer costs over €5
- **LATE** venues that stay open late (1am or after)
- our absolute favourites (>81)

maddogski.com

Méribel

Barometer

T +33 (0)4 79 00 41 06

Route de la Montée (next to the baker near the main square), 2pm-2am.

Convenient for the centre of the village, this spacious bar is slick in a low-key way and makes a nice change from some of the more grungy bars in resort. Staff either speak good English or are Brits funding their ski season. Comfortable seating and wooden panelling make it a good place to settle for a few cocktails before heading out for a late supper or some dancing. There are pool tables and a plasma screen for

Live music

Many bars have live music throughout the week. The bands that come and play the Alps are often surprisingly good and in great demand. Check out posters in resort and at the venues for details.

Dicks Tea Bar/Pizza Express > 82	Regular live music till late
Le Pub > 83	Largest live music venue for a big night out
Le Rond Point > 85	Live music most days from 5-7pm
Scott's > 84	A slightly calmer music scene
Lodge du Village > 84	Regular live music in Méribel-Village
La Tsaretta > 85	Small and relaxed but can get very lively

Our favourite bars and nightclubs

Barometer >80	A chilled place to relax after a day on the snow. Grown up atmosphere with a good range of drinks
Dicks Tea Bar >82	Just a great night out with plenty of dancing
Fify50 >82	Small local bar
Le Rond Point >83	Classic Méribel après-ski
La Taverne >84	Busy bar in the centre of the resort with lots going on
La Tsaretta >85	Late night drinking in Les Allues

major sports events but these don't take over. Coffee and snacks are also served.

Cactus café

T +33 (0)4 79 00 53 67

The Chaudanne, 8am-12am.
If there's a sporting event on and you're in the mood to watch, this is the place to go. Frequent happy hours, food all day, regular live music during early après-ski and reasonably priced pitchers of beer. Luckily it's close enough to the bus stop to watch for your next ride.

Food and drink Après-ski

maddogski.com

Dicks Tea Bar

T +33 (0)4 79 08 60 19
W dicksteabar.com

Route de Mussillon, next to Pizza Express, 10pm-3.30am.

If people can name one bar in Méribel, this is usually the one. The infamous bar/nightclub stands alone and is loud, vibrant and usually packed later in the evening. Various DJs play throughout the season and there are regular theme and stand up comedy nights. The club is in Mussillon, the small village between Méribel and Méribel-Village. You can either take the Méribel-Village bus from the Chaudanne/tourist office or walk along the main road (it takes about 10 minutes from the main square). If you eat at Pizza Express (> 75) or arrive before 11pm entrance is free. Things get going quite late but given that it's open till 3.30am, that's not a problem. Just don't expect to be on the first lift the next morning.

Fifty50

T +33 (0)4 79 07 78 15

Route de la Montée (near the Chaudanne).

This is a flexible little place that can bend itself to what you want – a quick drink and some salty snacks, a long session propping up the bar or (later, on busy nights) a bowl of chilli and some red wine. Popular with seasonaires. Tiny though it is, friendly staff make it easy to spend time here.

Jack's Bar

T +33 (0)4 79 00 30 94

Tremplin complex (lower level) on Route de la Montée, 11am-1am.

Basic bar with a welcoming atmosphere that attracts a young crowd. Head here for a few drinks and a game of pool. Snacks (pizzas and pies) are served. Roll the dice to beat bar staff and get your drink for free. Good early après-ski but can be quiet later on in the evening. The comedy nights are worth checking out.

Le Loft
T +33 (0)4 79 00 36 58

Parc Olympique, 10pm-4am.
Méribel's grown-up nightclub. Le Loft is a bit more French and sophisticated than Dick's but still accessible – and great fun on its theme evenings. It's also more centrally located; in the Parc Olympique building – entrance is via a side door (the side furthest from the piste).

Le Poste
T +33 (0)4 79 00 74 31

Main square (next to the tourist office), 10am-1.30am.
When you feel you've exhausted the budget venues, this is the place to head for. The cool, urban bar is particularly suitable for a few champagne cocktails (around €10) to start the night with. Alternatively have a demi or a kir. If you want to stick around then the music/DJ is usually good value and the view (the best-looking people in the resort) is splendid. Le Poste has a small terrace where you can enjoy a peaceful coffee during the day.

Le Pub
T +33 (0)4 79 08 60 02

Main square (by the tourist office), 4pm-1.30am.
Upbeat bar with live music pretty much every day and happy hour from 4-7pm. Noisy and busy but a lot of fun.

Le Rond Point
T +33 (0)4 79 00 37 51
W rondpointmeribel.com

At the Rond-Point (the area, though not the bar itself, is marked on your piste map), 9am-7pm.
A pivotal part of the Méribel après-ski experience (complete with toffee vodka) and especially popular with the Brits. The bar is ski in, ski out (reach it via **Marmotte** or **Rhodos**). Good vin chaud, a vibrant atmosphere plus live music

maddogski.com

from 5pm. The only problem is that it shuts up shop at 7pm but it's easy to get a bus back home. Alternatively, if you leave while it's still light you can ski the last stretch down into Méribel.

Scott's
T +33 (0)4 79 00 39 61

Main square, 4pm-1am.
This basement bar is a chilled place to relax, with low lighting and plenty of comfy seating. Things can kick off when there is live music (including dancing on the long-suffering sofas). ➤ 84.

La Taverne
T +33 (0)4 79 00 36 18
W lataverne-meribel.com

Main square (opposite the tourist office), 8am-1am.
Easy-going popular bar in the centre of the village. ➤ 84.

Mottaret
Annexe Bar
T +33 (0)4 79 04 06 10

In the main shopping area (next to Pizzeria du Mottaret), 8am-2am.
An antidote to the mountain's pine-and-log-fire establishments, should you need it. The friendly French owner has created a lively bar with an upbeat atmosphere.

Le Privilege
T: +33 (0)4 79 08 59 74

In the main shopping area (near Le Grenier restaurant), 11pm-3am.
The only true nightclub in Mottaret receives mixed reviews from punters. Can get busy in high season.

Méribel-Village
Lodge du Village
T: +33 (0)4 79 01 03 55

Centre of the village (ski access is by lapin), 11am-1am.

The choice of nightlife in Méribel-Village may be small but it packs a punch. LDV has regular live music (ask at the bar for details) during early après-ski and is a good general pub too. ➤ 80.

Les Allues
La Tsaretta
T +33 (0)4 79 08 61 00

Route des Carons, 5pm-1.30am.
A buzzing little place which is well worth a visit. Live music, dancing and you can even pop upstairs for a meal. ➤ 78.

Mountain restaurants
This section reviews every mountain restaurant shown on the Three Valleys piste maps, whether good, bad or indifferent (plus a few 'unofficial' ones).

Some at the bottom end of the restaurant list can be complacent, with unimaginative menus and pretty average food. Others make a real effort and even classics such as spag bol, carbonara and pizza are tasty and filling. However they almost all have stunning views, so even if we don't recommend their food, they can be great places to have a morning or afternoon break.

Almost every restaurant opens and closes with the pistes and lifts. Lunch is generally around 12-3pm, longer in high season. If you've got a place in mind, or you're part of a large group, we recommend you book, except in really quiet periods.

For the keen skier, self-service restaurants are a real bonus, especially when it's busy. They tend to have more flexible lunch hours, and as you can usually be fed and watered in under 30mins, you're free to ski during the quieter lunch period of 12-2pm. There are some surprisingly good self-service places in the Three Valleys and they're often the cheaper option.

Guide to our symbols ➤ 70.

Our favourite mountain restaurants

Adray Télébar > 93	Generous helpings from a varied menu. Delicious puddings
Le Rond Point > 95	Lively atmosphere great alternative to the traditional Savoyard fare
Le Cap Horn > 95	'The' place in Courchevel for an extravagant lunch
Les Chenus > 96	Good value self-service restaurant with a reasonable choice of dishes and a large terrace
Le Bel Air > 97	Fabulous views, welcoming service and simple food
Le Roc Tania > 99	Great location and good quality, traditional food
Les Sonnailles > 101	Good value food with a local flavour
Le Grand Lac > 101	Brilliant views complimented by quality food
Les Quatre Vents > 102	Interesting décor and a decent range of main courses
Le Chalet de Chavière > 104	Simple fare but one of the best views in the Alps
Le Chalet du Thorens > 105	Good choice and value for money

Restaurants

1. Les Pierres Plates
2. Les Rhododendrons
3. Le Choucas
4. Le Chardonnet
5. Côte 2000
6. Adray Télébar
7. La Sitelle
8. L'Arpasson
9. Le Mont de la Chambre
10. Le Chalet Togniat
11. Le Roc de 3 Marches
12. Les Crêtes

Restaurants

1. Le Bel Air
2. Le Casserole
3. Les Pierres Plates
4. Le Panoramic
5. Le Cap Horn
6. L'Altibar, Le Pilatus
7. L'Arc-en-ciel
8. Les Verdons
9. Le Chalet des Pierres
10. Les Chenus
11. La Soucoupe
12. Le Roc Tania
13. Le Bouc Blanc

Restaurants

1. Le Chardon Bleu
2. Corbeleys
3. La Loy
4. Le Roc de 3 Marches
5. Le Grand Lac
6. Le Chalet des Neiges
7. Chalet du Cairn
8. Mont de la Chambres
9. Les Quatres Vents
10. Le France/Chez Alfred
11. L'Alpage
12. Les Sonnailles
13. Les 3 V
14. Les Roches Blanches
15. Le Panoramic
16. La Ruade

Restaurants

1. Le Chalet Plein Sud
2. Le Chalet de Caron
3. Le Chalet de 2 Ours
4. L'Altiself 3000
5. Le Bar de la Marine
6. Le Chalet du Thorens
7. Le Chalet des 2 Lacs
8. La Moutiere
9. Le Chalet du Génépi
10. Le Chalet de Chavière
11. L'Etape 3200
12. Le Chalet Refuge Chinal Donat

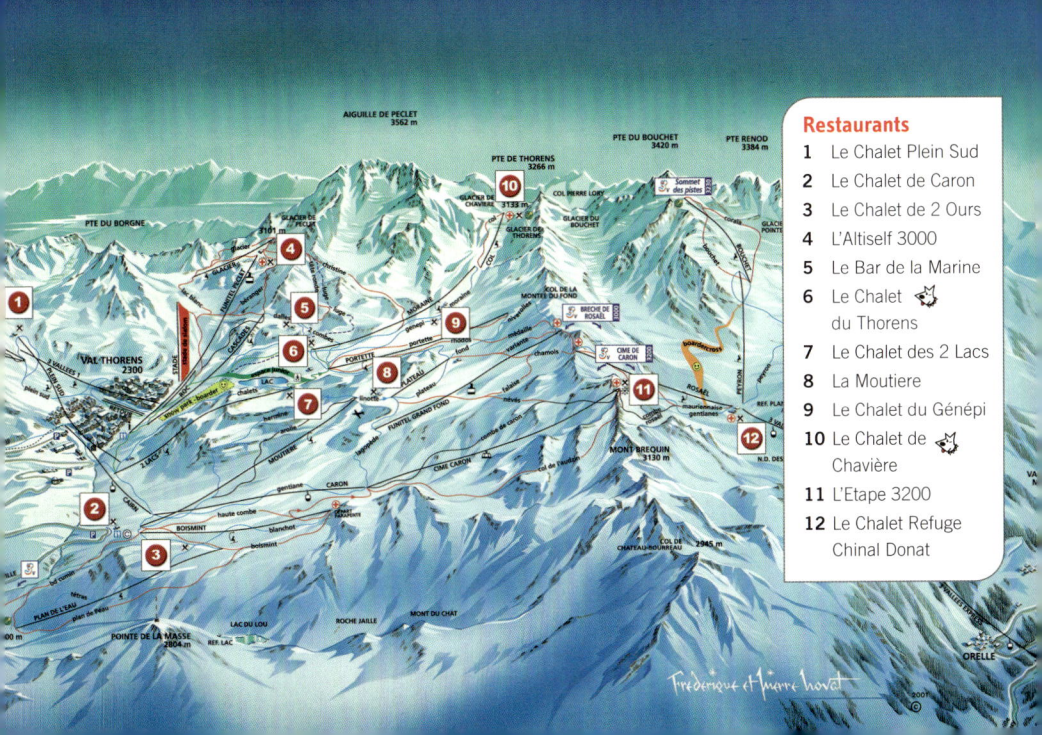

Finding your restaurant

in the Three Valleys and they're often the cheaper option.

Guide to our symbols > 70. In this section you'll find reviews for all of the restaurants marked on the official piste map that can be easily reached from Méribel. Rather unhelpfully, restaurants appear on the piste map as a knife and fork symbol, rather than by name. Mad Dog have created our own maps (>87 – 90) and numbered each restaurant. The number next to each of our reviews corresponds to the maps. You may also need to cross-refer to the larger piste map to navigate your way to your chosen restaurant.

Méribel also has some great places to eat that are not shown on the piste map but are very close to the pistes. We have reviewed the best ones. Don't forget that another option is to head back to the resort for lunch.

Where possible, we set out the best way for pedestrians to reach mountain restaurants. However, quite a few of the more remote ones (especially in resorts other than Méribel) are inaccessible unless you're on skis.

Méribel & Mottaret

Adray Télébar 6
T +33 (0)4 79 08 60 26

Lifts/pedestrian: Near the bottom of Adret, Rhodos 1 (pedestrians should walk across the piste from the Rond Point) or head down Doron.

A much-loved mountain restaurant. It's close to a number of lifts and pistes, so a good meeting place – definitely worth booking ahead. Helpings are generous and menu varied – asparagus with blue cheese, crozet with Reblochon, delicious veal (€12-35). The puddings are highly recommended and chips fantastic. The Télébar is also a lovely place to stop for a jug of vin chaud (€5). You can eat here in the evenings and even book into one of their hotel rooms.

L'Arpasson 8
T +33 (0)4 79 08 54 79

Lifts/pedestrian: Tougnète 1 or head down Grive, Faon or Ecureuil.
Good for non-skiers; sunny terrace, friendly staff and quick service. For a longer lunch try the upstairs restaurant.

Les Choucas 3
T +33 (0)4 79 00 58 31

Lifts/pedestrian: Burgin 1 (and a short but quite steep walk down – and back up) or head down Cerf.
Tucked away below Burgin mid station. Credit cards accepted over €15.

Les Crêtes 12
T +33 (0)4 79 08 56 50

Lifts/pedestrian: Tougnète 2 (top station) Tougnète Tsk or St Martin 2, then a walk along Crêtes.
A small but very friendly restaurant with amazing views over the Méribel and St Martin valleys.

Les Rhododendrons 2
T +33 (0)4 79 00 50 92

Lifts/pedestrian: Rhodos 2 or head down Blanchot.

Next to the beginners' area in Méribel and close to the walkers' trails around the Altiport area.

Le Chalet Togniat 10
T +33 (0)4 79 00 45 11

Lifts: Combes, alternatively ski down Martre or Lagopède, Pedestrian: no access.
Modern restaurant with an old chalet feel. Self-service and restaurant options. Sunny terrace in the afternoon.

Le Chardonnet 4
T +33 (0)4 79 00 44 81

Lifts/pedestrian: Pas du Lac 1, or take Marcassin or Niverolle.
Great views of the Méribel valley, interesting menu and friendly staff. Worth booking ahead.

Côte 2000 5
T +33 (0)4 79 00 55 40

Lifts: Ramées from Mottaret or take Aiglon, Pedestrian: no access.
A reasonably priced mountain restaurant with most meals under €14. Self-service but your food is brought to your table. Examples of the plat du jour includes confit du canard (€15). The restaurant is a lovely place to stop for lunch and one of our researcher's favourite places – the staff are always friendly and it has great views and location.

Les Pierres Plates 1
T +33 (0)4 79 00 42 38

Lifts/pedestrian: Burgin 2, Pas du Lac 2. Also a short ski down from Saulire.
Handy location to meet non-skiers. However, food is average and not cheap.

La Sitelle 7
T +33 (0)4 79 00 43 48

Lifts/pedestrian: Plattières 1 or head down Martre.
This relaxed simple restaurant serves typical Savoyard food but service can be slow on busy days.

Le Blanchot
(not on piste map)
T +33 (0)4 79 00 55 78

*Lifts/pedestrian: Golf (walk goes via Altiport road and also cross-country tracks) or take **Blanchot**.*
Another good place to meet non-skiing friends. Booking essential.

Le Rond point
(not on piste map)
T +33 (0)4 79 00 37 51

*Lifts/pedestrian: Rhodos mid station (alternatively walk from Méribel) or head down **Marmotte** or **Rhodos**.*
Deservedly one of the most popular bars and restaurants in Méribel, which transforms into a lively après-ski venue with regular live music. The food is a breath of fresh air from the standard Savoyard fare – fish, stir-fry and pasta are all available. Snack bars outside on the terrace and also downstairs sell a range of quick eats; paninis (€6), chips (€5), burgers/chicken/sandwiches (€8).

Courchevel 1850
L'Altibar, Le Pilatus 6
T +33 (0)4 79 08 20 49

*Pistes: **Pralong, Altiport**, Pedestrian: Altiport shuttle bus.*
Next to the airport, this is Courchevel's answer to Heathrow's viewing gallery. Children's menu available.

L'Arc-en-ciel 7
T +33 (0)4 79 08 38 09

*Pistes: **Combe de Saulire, Combe Pylônes, M**, Pedestrian: Verdons.*
Handy watering hole at 1850 mid-station. Friendly service and consistently good food. If you pre-book avoid the mezzanine floor as it doesn't have a view.

Le Cap Horn 5
T +33 (0)4 79 08 33 10

Lifts/pedestrian: Take the Altiport lift (shuttle bus for pedestrians) or head down *Pralong* or *Altiport*. 'The' place in Courchevel for an extravagant lunch. If you can't stretch to lunch, take a drink stop to watch the beautiful (and well-heeled) people of Courchevel. The famous 'plateau' Cap Horn (€110 for two) has every shellfish you can imagine. Or choose an 'appellation controllé' Bresse chicken, €95. Salads are €17-32 and pasta €23-38.

Le Chalet de Pierres 9
T +33 (0)4 79 08 18 61

Pistes: Verdons, Pedestrian: Via G2 Jardin Alpin, requires a short walk.
Not cheap, but their dessert buffet is legendary (€16). The side bar has crêpes and snacks for around €3-6.

Les Chenus 10
T +33 (0)4 79 08 06 84

Lifts/pedestrian: Chenus (with a short walk uphill), Coqs, Crêtes then take Col de la Loze (requires a short walk uphill).
A large and airy restaurant that gets our vote for being probably the best value self-service in Courchevel, and with a large and sunny terrace. Main courses are between €8.50-21.50, and there's a good choice of snacks, pasta and simple dishes.

Le Panoramic 4
T +33 (0)4 79 08 00 88

Lifts/pedestrian: Saulire or Burgin-Saulire and Pas du Lac (short walk uphill).

The first floor restaurant serves Savoyard classics along with other less common mountain dishes such as 'chest of pig' enameled with spices (€25). A more basic self-service is downstairs.

La Soucoupe Restaurant 11
T +33 (0)4 79 08 21 34

Lifts/pedestrian: Planetrey, Loze, Bouc Blanc, Chenus (with a 10 minute walk down Crêtes, returning the same way) or take Crêtes or Loze Est.

The restaurant is a perennial favourite, with a cosy wooden chalet feel for colder days or the fabulously sunny terrace with views of 1850. The delicious food and excellent service contrasts with the quality of food offered in the self-service downstairs, although the panini and snack bar are good value. Try the grilled lamb chops with thyme (€28) or duck breast in honey (€26).

Les Verdons 8
T +33 (0)4 79 08 38 04

Lifts/pedestrian: Verdons, Pedestrian: Sources, Rocher de l'Ombre or ski down Combe de Saulire or Combe Pylônes.

The food is disappointing, staff aren't that friendly and it's not that cheap either – save this one just for drinks breaks. Eat at l'Arc-en-ciel next door.

Courchevel 1650
Le Bel Air 1
T +33 (0)4 79 08 00 93

Lifts/pedestrian: Ariondaz (pedestrian), Bel Air or take Grand Bosses, Ariondaz, Pyramide or Rochers – halfway down.

Fabulous views, three sunny terraces and very friendly (English speaking) service. Food is simple but good quality. Roast chicken or pork chops and chips (€17.50), and a choice of pasta (€13.50). Generally main courses range between €13.50-31.

In high season they serve a full menu until 3.30pm, but will still offer omelettes, salads and other lighter dishes pretty much until closing time. Booking essential.

La Casserole 2
T +33 (0)4 79 08 06 35

Lifts: Marquis (with a short walk), 3 Vallées or take Grandes Bosses or Ariondaz.
In direct contrast to its friendly neighbour, Le Bel Air. Although the food is similarly priced, the service is miles apart. If you're planning to eat in 1650, book Le Bel Air (which also has better views).

L'Ours Blanc
(not on piste map)
T +33 (0)4 79 00 93 93

Situated at the bottom of the runs into 1650.
Typical menu of burgers, pasta, and Savoyard cuisine. Situated at the bottom of the runs in 1650. No reservations.

La Tania

Le Bouc Blanc 13
T +33 (0)4 79 08 80 26

Lifts/pedestrian: La Tania lift. Alternatively head down Dou des Lanches, Jockeys, Lanches, Bouc Blanc or Arolles.
This is one of the best value mountain restaurants with friendly service, good size portions of tasty food and a handy stop before hitting La Tania. In early season the north-facing terrace only gets sun from mid-morning till early afternoon. The hot Beaufort tart with salad is excellent (€10) and is big enough as a main, or try the three course menu for €18. Children welcome (€10 for two courses).

Le Roc Tania 12
T +33 (0)4 79 08 32 34

*Lifts/pedestrian: **Dou des Lanches**, La Tania (both pedestrian), Loze, Col de la Loze.*

A great place to finish a week's skiing with drinks on the terrace and amazing views. From here you can ski home pretty much anywhere other than 1650. The menu has all the usual suspects, all well cooked and presented. Options include tagliatelle with Roquefort and walnuts (€13.70) and free range roast chicken (€17.90). A nice touch is the baskets they provide for your gloves, hats and goggles.

Children's menu €12.90 (two courses).

Pub Le Ski Lodge
Lively restaurant serving English pub-type food at the bottom of Folyères. Sunny terrace.

St Martin de Belleville
Le Chardon Bleu 1
T +33 (0)4 79 08 95 36

Lift/pedestrians: Take St Martin 1 and ski down Verdet or Pelozet.
Sunny terrace, good food and reliable service.

Le Corbeleys 2
T +33 (0)4 79 08 95 31

Lift/pedestrians: Take St Martin 1 and ski down Verdet or Pelozet.
Small but relaxed restaurant with a terrace complete with deck chairs for sunny days and limited seating indoors for colder days. Excellent value food although the menu isn't large; typical Savoyard dishes – tartiflette, crozzeflette (€9 -15). Wine by the glass starts from €2.20. The dish of the day is usually great.

maddogski.com

La Loy 3
T +33 (0)4 79 08 92 72

Lift/pedestrian s: Take St Martin 1 and ski down Biolley.
Slightly off the main piste on the way into St Martin, though still accessible on skis.

La Bouitte
(not on piste map)
T +33 (0)4 79 08 96 77

St Marcel offers a gastronomic Michelin-starred experience. Reservations essential. They will send a mini bus to collect you from St Martin if snow conditions don't allow you to ski there. Don't come here if you're not up for a long lunch (and don't miss the last lifts home).

Les Menuires
L'Alpage 11
T +33 (0)4 79 00 75 16

Lifts: Take Montaulever lift and ski down Mont de la Chambre or 4 vents, Pedestrian: no access.
Range of food to suit most tastes and based in a quiet location. Sun terrace for warmer days.

Le Chalet du Cairn 7
T +33 (0)4 79 00 19 81

Lifts: Take Mont de la Chambre lift and ski down Liason or David Douillet, Pedestrian: no access.
Large outside terrace for dining on sunny days, as well as deckchairs for a relaxing drink.

Le Chalet des Neiges 6
T +33 (0)4 79 00 60 55

Lifts/Pedestrian: Take the Roc des 3 marche lift and ski down Petits Creux or Combes.
The Chalet des Neiges has excellent, reasonably priced food

(main course €8.50-12) in a great atmosphere. Friendly staff offer a quick service complimented by the lovely terrace on which to soak up the sun on lazy afternoons. Kids menu available.

Les Sonnailles 12
T +33 (0)4 79 00 74 28

Pistes: Boulevard Cumin, Pedestrian: Just off Bruyères and a short walk from the road.
Sitting with a cluster of other farm buildings on the left as you ski into Les Menuires on the beautiful (and easy) Boulevard Cumin. Order at the counter, and your food is then delivered to your table. The menu is good value and, combined with such a lovely old building, this is a must. Booking is essential (also open most evenings except Sunday and Monday).

La Ruade 16
T +33 (0)4 79 00 61 06

Lifts/pedestrian: Just below Les Menuires – follow signs for Tortollet and Rocher Noir.
Pretty little chalet-type restaurant just below Les Menuires with views up the valley and over La Masse, serving local dishes and a children's menu.

Le France aka Chez Alfred 10
T +33 (0)4 79 00 67 79

Lifts/pedestrian: Take the Reberty lift and ski down Boyes or Mont de la Chambre (just a short walk from Reberty lift for pedestrians).
This restaurant needs a bit of TLC but food is cheap and cheerful, with friendly staff and efficient service.

Le Grand Lac 5
T +33 (0)4 79 08 25 78

Lifts: Ski down the Gros Tougne or Teppes runs, Pedestrian: no access.
Views up towards Les Menuires valley and down to St Martin.

maddogski.com

Despite the size, it still manages to feel cosy and authentic. The food is good quality and service is friendly and efficient. Well worth stopping for a nice long, lazy lunch.

Le Mont de la Chambre 8
T +33 (0)4 79 00 67 68

Lifts/pedestrian: Bruyères 2 (pedestrians should come from the top of the Bruyères bubble), Mont de la Chambre, Côte Brune.
Self-service is great for a quick, reasonably priced lunch. Don't leave without trying the BBQ smelt (€14). The restaurant is more expensive. Terrace views mainly blocked by lift buildings.

Le Panoramic 15
T +33 (0)4 79 22 80 60

Lifts: Masse 2, Pedestrian: no access.
One of the best views in the Three Valleys, so it's a shame the restaurant isn't better.

Les Quatre Vents 9
T +33 (0)4 79 00 64 44

Lifts: Take Bruyères 1 and head down Liaison, Mont de la Chambre or 4 vents, Pedestrian: no access.
This restaurant is decked out with very French décor and comes with bags of atmosphere; there's a display of labelled stuffed animals to interest both kids and adults alike, as you don't see much wildlife in the winter. The food is standard but good and freshly made. Great terrace for sunny days and large indoor area when the weather's not so nice. Good place to meet non-skiers.

Le Roc des 3 Marches 4
T +33 (0)4 79 00 46 48

Lifts/pedestrian: Allamands, Granges, Plattières 3 (pedestrians take a short walk from here).
Good meeting point. Limited menu but efficient service.

Les Roches Blanches 14
T +33 (0)4 79 00 60 22

🪙

Lifts/pedestrian: Take Masses 1 and ski down Vallons.

Good drink stop before you tackle La Masse but prices aren't cheap. Non-customers have to pay to use the toilets.

Les 3 V 13
T +33 (0)4 79 00 60 22

🪙

Lifts: Bd Enverse, Vallons, Pedestrian: no access

Handy place to stop on the way down Le Masse with views towards Cime de Caron from the terrace.

Val Thorens

L'Altiself 3000 4
T + 33 (0)4 79 00 03 76

🪙 V

Lifts/Pedestrian: Take the Funitel or Peclet lift up and ski down

Béranger.
Self-service (€8.60-15) and restaurant (€14-30).

Food and drink Mountain restaurants

103

Le Bar de la Marine 5
T + 33 (0)4 79 00 03 12

Lifts: Take the Cascades lift up and come down Les Dalles or Tête ronde, Pedestrian: no access.
Upstairs restaurant is more formal and on the expensive side. Downstairs it couldn't be more different – cheap and cheerful with a limited menu.

Le Chalet de 2 Ours 3
T + 33 (0)4 79 01 14 09

Pistes: Blanchot, Pedestrian: no access.
Nice sundeck for warmer weather. Reasonable vegetarian options and a kid's menu. The interior is filled with bears – hence the name – which will keep the kids amused.

Le Chalet de Caron 2
T + 33 (0)4 79 00 01 71

Lifts: At the bottom of the Boismint, Caron and Mouitiere lifts. Pedestrian: A short walk from Val Thorens.
Large restaurant but busy especially on sunny days. Terrace with deckchairs. Children's menu.

Le Chalet de Chavière 10

Lifts: Col, Pedestrian: no access.
This tiny mountain refuge at 3120m wins our vote for one of the best views in the Alps. However there has been uncertainty about whether it will re-open this year or not. If you do find it open, there are only two choices on the menu – soup of the day (€7) or a meat, cheese and bread platter (€9). Their small outside area has deck chairs, picnic tables and benches. There are no toilets, and take some cash as credit cards are not accepted.

Le Chalet du Thorens 6
T + 33 (0)4 79 00 02 80

Pistes: 2 Combes, Moraine.

Located at a busy junction with an oversized plastic knife and fork on the roof, this restaurant is difficult to miss. The views are not as good as some of the higher restaurants and the décor isn't brilliant, but it gets our vote for choice and value. Restaurant dishes include fresh pasta and leg of pork with warm lentils (€15). The outside terrace has a cover for colder weather. Downstairs, the self-service café cooks fresh pasta to order and there's also a salad bar. Snacks are available outside for €6-8.

Le Chalet des 2 Lacs 7
T + 33 (0)4 79 00 28 54

Lifts: Les Deux Lacs, Pedestrian: no access.

This popular, friendly restaurant gets very busy so be prepared to queue for the outside snack bar if you're in a rush. Restaurant is reasonably priced and the menu offers the usual mountain fare – pastas, tarts, cured meat platters, salads from €9-18. Good sunny terrace and deckchairs. Kids menu available, and a good location for the little ones to ski back into Val Thorens. They don't take reservations so it's best to come early or late.

Le Chalet du Génépi 9
T + 33 (0)4 79 00 03 28
Pistes: Génépi.

Cosy interior which makes it look smaller than it is. Food is simple (pasta, chips etc), and because of the location it can get busy, so arrive early.

Le Chalet Refuge Chinal Donat 12
T + 33 (0)4 79 56 53 01

*Lifts: Take the 3 Vallées express and ski down Gentianes or **Combes Roaël/Mauriennaise**, Mauriennaise, Pedestrian: no access.*

The only restaurant in the fourth valley. The menu is nothing special but the food freshly made and quite cheap. Credit cards over €10.

Le Chalet Plein Sud 1
T + 33 (0)4 79 00 04 27

Lifts: Plein Sud, Pedestrian: no access.

Standard mountain restaurant menu but cheap prices. Large indoor and outdoor seating areas with good views over Val Thorens.

L'Etape 3200 11
T + 33 (0)6 07 31 04 14

Lifts: Cime Caron cable car, Pedestrian: no access.

The highest restaurant in the Three Valleys, with views into the fourth valley and Italy. Unremarkable menu but good quality – we recommend the spaghetti bolognaise. Worth a visit for the views, but avoid the toilets if you can wait.

La Moutiere 8
T + 33 (0)4 79 00 02 67

Lifts: Take the Moutiere lift and ski down Plateau. Pedestrian: no access.

Relatively small but homely restaurant. Food is simple but good; ham, egg and chips, chicken and chips etc. Snacks and drinks also available from the window outside.

Can't ski? Won't ski? Too much snow or not enough..? Find out about the **other things to do** in Méribel.

What you'll find in this chapter

Non-skiing activities. 107
Shopping............................... 115
The map (➤ 6) shows the shopping areas

Whether lack of snow has driven you off the slopes, you're a non-skier or you simply feel like a change, there are loads of things to do in Méribel.

One of the resort's greatest, though perhaps not most beautiful, assets is the Parc Olympique – the sports centre on the edge of the Chaudanna map (➤ 6). Here, you can do a range of activities including ice skating, climbing and swimming. If you or your children are particularly energetic, you can add a special swimming pool and ice-rink option to your ski pass. The cost for six days is €25 for adults / €17.50 for children. Further price details are below.

Art and Exhibitions

The tourist office in Méribel hosts various exhibitions. Pick up their 'Highlights of the week' leaflet for details. There is also a small museum in Les Allues with exhibitions on the area's history.
T +33 (0)4 79 00 59 08
Tuesday and Thursday, 2-6.30pm, free.

Beauty and Therapies
Aspen Park Hotel
T +33 (0)4 79 00 99 09
Rond-Point.
This Club Med hotel spa offers a variety of massages, wraps and scrubs. By appointment only, **Le Ludicur** (below) is more convenient for Méribel town centre.

Le Ludicoff Hairdresser
T +33 (0)4 79 08 89 07
Route de la Montée (in Hotel La Chaudanne), 9.30am-12.30pm, 2.00-7.30pm.

Le Ludicur Spa
T +33 (0)4 79 08 89 08
9am–8pm Monday to Saturday Route de la Montée (in Hotel

Other things to do

Chaudanne).
Offers various beauty treatments. Squash courts also available.

Parc Olympique
T +33 (0)4 79 00 58 21
2pm-7.15pm (9.15pm on Tuesdays and Thursdays).
A well-deserved sauna, Jacuzzi and steam room package will cost you €13 per person (over 15s only). Towels can be rented for an additional €3.10.

Pamper off Piste
T +33 (0)6 17 60 89 02
W pamperoffpiste.com
Beauty therapists will visit your chalet, apartment or hotel to provide a range of good quality beauty treatments including manicures, pedicures and facials. Massages range in price from €42 to €93, but discounts are available for group bookings.

Bowling
T +33 (0)4 79 00 36 44
Parc Olympique, 2pm-2am (early opening from 11am in bad weather).

A six-lane bowling alley complete with electronic boards, games, video screens and bar. Specially adapted shoes and bowls are available for children. Pre-booking is available (and advisable) during high season.

Cinema
Méribel
T +33 (0)8 92 68 73 33
W cinealpes.fr
Galerie des Cimes.

On the right-hand side of Route du Centre as you walk up the mountain away from the tourist office. There are usually two films per evening with an extra showing in the afternoon if the weather is bad. You'll find film listings in the tourist office's 'Highlights of the week' leaflet, or from the cinema itself. English films are advertised as 'VOST' (original version with French sub-titles).

SKIPHYSIQUE

LUXURY ALPINE FITNESS SOLUTIONS

We offer a bespoke and fully mobile Physique training service to exclusive guests in Courchevel and Méribel. Qualified personal trainers will visit you in the privacy of your own chalet.

For keen skiers our pre and Apres stretch package will ensure that you get the most out of your time on the mountain.

Whatever your needs, our highly skilled trainers have a treatment to soothe aching limbs and replenish energy levels.

- Yoga
- Pilates
- Boxing
- Tone it up
- Apres Stretch
- Hula
- Swiss Ball
- Physique body and mind
- Jane Fonda workout
- Learn to swim
- Aqua

bookings@skiphysique.com • www.skiphysique.com • UK: +44(0)7920 163 154 • FR: +33 (0)684 373 692

Mottaret

In the tourist office building > 143. Listings and showings are as above.

Climbing

T +33 (0)4 79 00 30 38
Parc Olympique, *9am-6pm (until 8.30pm at weekends).*

    Experienced climbers can use this indoor climbing wall free of charge. Tuition (from €6 per climb) and ice-climbing can also be arranged. To check availability and for tuition information, contact the Mountain Guides Office at the Parc Olympique. > 26.

Flights

Méribel Air

T +33 (0)4 79 01 10 22
Around €80 per person for a 20 minute flight.

    Take a tour of the Three Valleys in a light aircraft.

Go-karting on ice

Sports Loisirs des Montagnes

T +33 (0)6 11 27 76 72
Parc Olympique, *Mondays from 7.30-10pm, €20 for 10 minutes.*

Hot air ballooning

Ski Vol

T +33 (0)4 79 08 41 72
Around €220 per flight.
From various locations.

Ice skating *('Patinoire')*

T +33 (0)4 79 00 58 21
Parc Olympique, 2pm (4pm on Wednesdays) -7.30pm (9.30pm on Tuesdays and Thursdays). Children €3.10 (5-13, under 5s go free) and adults €4.60. Skate hire €3.10.

    Large, indoor rink with a café by the side for those who would rather watch.

Paintballing

T +33 (0)6 75 48 76 30
A 100-pellet package in a specially equipped area costs €20.

Paragliding *(parapenting)*

Various companies arrange trips over the valley – you should telephone beforehand as departure points depend on weather conditions. Expect to pay around €80 per person for a tandem flight with a qualified instructor:

A-Erodynamique Parapent
- **T** +33 (0)6 09 92 25 80 or
- **T** +33 (0)4 79 00 48 09,
- **W** parapentemeribailes.com

Craig's paragliding
- **T** +33 (0)4 79 08 43 65 or
- **T** +33 (0)6 81 64 69 70

From Bouc Blanc (at the top of Plantrey TS) and under Cretes TS.

Ski Vol
- **T** +33 (0)6 83 97 53 26
- **W** skivol.com

From the top of Vizelle and from Col de la Loze.

Skidoos
Snow Biker
- **T** +33 (0)4 79 00 40 01
- **W** snow-biker.com

Based in Mottaret.
One hour outings from €75 (plus €20 for additional passenger).

Special packages available for children (€10 for 10 minutes).

Shopping

For details of Méribel shops > 115.

For serious spending, head over to Courchevel 1850 for a wider choice of more upmarket shops. The three main shopping areas are Le Forum, Espace Diamant (extemely expensive) and the streets around La Croisette.

If you need a break, pop into **Le Chocolaté** on Rue Park City. €7 buys you bowls of molten chocolate, whipped cream and a jug of milk to make your own chocolate heaven.

Other things to do

maddogski.com

Sledging / luge

You can buy sledges and bum boards in most ski hire shops around the resort. The most popular sledging area for children is at the Rond-Point where there is also a moving carpet. You can reach it by bus from Méribel (direction 'Altiport') or by taking the Rhodos bubble from the Chaudanne and getting off at the first stop. The Altiport area is also suitable for sledging.

Teenagers and adults looking for a challenge may want to take the luge run from Courchevel 1850 to 1550. It starts from the top of the Tovets chairlift behind La Croisette – marked on the piste map in yellow. The only floodlit sled-run in France, the luge is about two kilometres long, descending 300m with an average slope of 15%. It's open from 9am-7.30pm (depending on snow conditions). There's no charge but you will need to rent a sledge from one of the larger hire shops, which will cost around €5 for an afternoon.

After you've done the run you can take the Grangettes lift back up to 1850. Alternatively, a good place to end up for a cosy drink and meal in Courchevel 1550 is the tiny **L'Oeil de Boeuf**.

Based on Rue des Rois at the bottom of Tovets, it's about five minutes walk from where the luge run ends. You'll need to get a taxi back to Méribel afterwards (> 19). It should cost you around €25.

Snow-shoe hiking (racquettes à neige) and walking

The tourist office can give you a map of groomed walking paths, many of which take you through breathtaking, silent woods that show a very different side of the Alps in winter.

You can also purchase a pedestrian lift-pass which entitles you to lift access and use of the in-resort buses in both Méribel and Courchevel (€14 per day or €41 for six days). It does not cover the Pass Montagne bus route that links Méribel and Courchevel. Ask at the lift-pass offices for further details.

Hiking boots are fine for shorter walks on groomed trails. However, if you're going into wilder country with deeper snow, we recommend hiring snow-shoes from a good ski-rental shop. And for longer outings, why not join a guided walk:

ESF
T +33 (0)4 79 08 60 31
W esf-meribel.com

Raquett'Evasion
T +33 (0)4 79 24 10 40
W raquettevasion.com
Various excursions including half and full day outings. Information can be obtained from the Twinner shops in Méribel (near the pharmacy) and the Rond-Point and Superski-Ski Set in Mottaret.

maddogski.com

Snow-making facility tours

T +33 (0)4 79 08 65 32

If you're intrigued by how they make artificial snow then go on a tour: 5pm every Wednesday.

Swimming pool

T +33 (0)4 79 00 58 21

Parc Olympique, 2pm-7.15pm (until 9.15pm on Tuesdays and Thursdays). Children under five go free, ages 5-13 €3.40, adults €4.30. Frequent use packages available. Sauna/steam room/Jacuzzi €13, towel rental €3.10.

The highlights of the Parc Olympique include a 25-metre pool, an excellent slide (minimum age six) and a baby pool. For an additional charge you can use the relaxing area with sauna, steam room and Jacuzzi (over 15s only). If you visit on a sunny day you'll probably have it pretty much to yourself.

The lovely heated outdoor pool by the Parc Olympique is sadly only for those staying in Hôtels La Chaudanne, L'Eterlou and Le Tremplin.

Walks

See **snow-shoe hiking > 113**.

Other events

Weekly events are detailed in the 'Highlights of the Week' leaflet, available from the tourist office. Also look out for posters in bars and around the resort.

Whitetracks

T +33 (0)6 86 12 34 17 or
T +33 (0)6 21 45 08 90
W whitetracks.co.uk

This English-run company, based in Méribel, can organise a whole range of non-skiing activities for you, including paragliding, snowmobile riding, dog sledging and heli-skiing. Contact them via their website for further information.

Animation Services

T +33 (0)4 79 22 01 07
W animationservices.net

This company can arrange various events including torch-lit descents and dinner in mountain retreats.

Shopping

The resort has a good selection of shops, although prices are higher than at home. Most are in Méribel itself – as you come into the resort from Mussillon you will see food shops such as the Spar and Cooperative Laitière on the left-hand side. However, the real shopping starts a little further up at the 'Croix de Verdon' area by the flagpoles.

With occasional breaks, shops line the road from there all the way along Route de la Montée to the Chaudanne, and snake up the Route du Centre and Route de Morel towards the Rond-Point. The main shopping centres are the Tremplin complex, around the Parc Olympique, and the Galerie des Cimes (where the cinema is) on Route du Centre.

In Mottaret, most of the shops are clustered around the tourist office at the bottom of the piste. There are also shops in Châtelet, which is at the other end of the central piste area, around Hotel Mont-Vallon. In 1600, the Rond-Point, Méribel Village and Les Allues, the shopping is more limited but will generally cater for those forgotten essentials. And, wherever you're staying, you won't be too far from a ski rental shop.

Equipment hire and purchase ➤ 33.

Courchevel 1850 offers a more Parisian (and pricey) shopping experience, which is great for browsing.

Opening hours

Generally, shops are open every day from about 9.30am to 7pm. Quite a few close for two or three hours at lunchtime (although they may stay open right through at weekends). Hours can vary a little depending on weather and busy periods.

Equipment and clothes

While the choice of ski clothes and equipment is undeniably better in Méribel than in most UK shopping centres, don't expect to find too many bargains – unless you're prepared to wait for the end of season winter stock sales. The best way to find what you want is to take a wander around – even in the centre this won't take more than an hour or so. A lot of the shops stock very similar items, the ones listed below are a little bit different, better or just bigger.

Méribel
Sport Boutique
T +33 (0)4 79 08 63 00
Main Square – the large shop to your right as you stand facing the tourist office.
8.30am-12.30pm, 3-7.30pm (8.30am-7.30pm weekends),
Upmarket ski wear from Prada and the rest. Ski Set rental is downstairs. They have outlets in Le Plateau and the Belvédère area.

Georges Mauduit
T +33 (0)4 79 08 63 08
Route du Centre – to your left as you stand facing Le Poste bar near the tourist office.
8.30am-12.30pm, 3-7.30pm,
Upmarket clothing and equipment.

Odlo
Route du Centre – just up the hill from Georges Mauduit,
9am-12pm, 3-7pm.
Odlo has a good selection of thermal underwear. It's in the same row of shops as **Stéphanya**, which sells some pretty jewellery and gifts.

White Stuff
T +33 (0)4 79 00 38 75
Route du Centre, in the Galerie L'Arolaz on the right-hand side of the road, a short walk up from the tourist office 10am-12pm, 3-8pm.
Classic casual surf/ski bum clothing. Sugar is next door and also worth a visit.

Fat Face
T +33 (0)4 79 00 39 17
Route du Centre, In the Galerie des Cimes. 10am-12pm, 3-8pm.
Classic casual clothing. **White Spirit**, **O Shop** and **Intersport** are in the same complex.

Mad Dog Ski Méribel

Quiksilver

T +33 (0)4 79 08 53 72
Route du Centre, On the left-hand side up the hill away from Hotel Le Roc, 8.30am-12.30pm, 2.30-7.30pm.

Good selection of clothes including Quiksilver and Roxy.

Freeride

T +33 (0)4 79 00 52 21
W freeride.fr
Route de la Montée, *In the Tremplin complex, above Jack's Bar, 9am-12pm, 2-7.30pm.*

Wide choice of equipment alongside good accessories.

Mottaret
Olympic Ski

T +33 (0)4 79 00 48 51
At the bottom of the slopes near the tourist office. 8.30am-7.30pm.

Blanc Sports

T *+33 (0)4 79 00 44 07*
Châtelet area, near Hotel Mont-Vallon.

Stocks skis and boards as well as clothes from Quiksilver and Roxy. Ski Espace and Superski are in the same area.

Méribel-Village
Ski Set

T +33 (0)4 79 01 13 38
In the ski-lift area, 8.30am-12pm, 2-7pm.

Les Allues
Ski Higher

T +33 (04) 79 00 36 80
Route de la Rèse, near the supermarket, 8.30am-12pm, 3.30-7.30pm (8am-8pm at weekends).

Reasonably priced ski hire (used by some chalet companies) and essential clothing items.

Other things to do

Food and wine

Supermarkets and delicatessens

Supermarkets can be found throughout the resort. Opening hours are usually 8.30am-1pm and 4-7.30pm. Some offer a delivery service (with a charge of about €8 or free if you spend over €100) – ask for details if you're interested. As always, the prices in resort are significantly higher than in Moûtiers. If you have any 'can't live without' foods, like Marmite and English teabags, you're better off bringing them with you.

Sherpa supermarkets offer a pre-ordering system on sherpa.net, although you may find it difficult to use if you don't speak reasonable French. A good English website is **chaletfood.com** (+33 (0)4 79 38 30 68), who will purchase food for you.

The 'traiteurs' (delicatessens) are often a good bet if you're self-catering, though a little pricey. Many of them offer prepared home-cooked meals that just need re-heating.

Most of the supermarkets and delis sell a selection of wine. If you're keen to try a local vintage, ➤ 68 for more information.

Moûtiers

You'll find a Hyper Champion and a Super U in Moûtiers. The Champion is on the left as you drive into town from Albertville, while the Super U (slightly smaller) is on the right as you leave town, driving towards Méribel and Courchevel.

Méribel
Casino
T +33 (04) 79 08 54 26
Route de Mussillon, on the right-hand side as you walk from Hotel Le Roc towards Mussillon, 8.30am-12.30pm, 3.30-7.30pm.

Smaller than the Spar (see below) but more central.

Spar
T +33 (0)4 79 08 54 26
Route de Mussillon, on the right-hand side between Méribel and Mussillon, opposite the small stone church. Approximately 10 minutes' walk from the town centre. There's

a car park just before you reach the shop, 8.30am-1pm, 3-8pm.

Large-ish supermarket with a good selection of food and wine, plus towels, sunglasses, postcards etc. They also do take-away pizzas (+33 (0)4 79 00 32 32). The **Cooperative Laitière,** which sells local cheeses, meats and wines, is just after the Spar as you head away from the town centre.

Superette des Cimes
T +33 (0)4 79 08 65 18
Route du Centre, on the balcony in the Galerie des Cimes, 8am-12.45pm, 3-7.45pm.

General supermarket goods including meat, vegetables and wine. If you are doing your shopping here, pick up some cheese from La Fromagerie (see below).

La Fromagerie
T +33 (0)4 79 08 55 48
Route du Centre, in the Galerie des Cimes, 10am-12.30pm, 4.30-7.30pm.

Fantastic selection of cheese. In the evening, there is a fondue restaurant downstairs.

Traiteur Gourmand
T +33 (0)4 79 00 53 30
Route de Mussillon, 10am-8pm.

Take-away sandwiches and delicatessen goods including regional produce and cheese.

Plateau

Casino
T +33 (04) 79 08 54 26
In the main row of shops, 8am-12.30pm, 4.30-7.30pm.

Boucherie du Plateau, the butcher, and **Maison Braissand Les Flocons**, the baker, are nearby so you can do all your shopping at once.

1600

Sherpa
T +33 (0)6 32 44 27 86
Near the Méribel 1600 bus stop, 8.30am-12.30pm, 4-8pm.

General supermarket. Home delivery available. Rents out raclette / fondue equipment.

Mottaret

Sherpa
T +33 (0)4 79 00 40 91
In the main shopping area, 8am-12.30pm, 3.30-7.30pm.
　　Supermarket with useful staples such as fresh bread and spit-roast whole chickens.

8 à Huit
T +33 (0)4 79 00 45 56
In the Châtelet area near the bus stop.

Méribel-Village
Spar
T +33 (0)4 79 08 51 58
8am-12.30pm, 4-7.30pm.
　　Supermarket, general goods, phonecards etc. Delivery service available. Bureau de change facilities.

Les Allues
Vival
T +33 (0)4 79 08 62 81
Route de la Rèse, *8am-12.30pm, 4.30-7.30pm.*

Bakers
　　France is renowned for its fabulous range of bread and pastries – and Méribel is no exception. Bakers often sell tasty picnic food such as filled baguettes, slices of pizza and apple tarts – perfect for al fresco dining on the slopes.

Méribel
Maison Braissand Les Glaciers
T +33 (0)4 79 08 60 27
Route de la Montée, Near the main square, diagonally across the road from Hotel Le Roc and La Taverne.
　　Good croissant, bread and cakes. They sell tasty pre-made sandwiches, and there's a Salon de Thé upstairs.

Patisserie de Ravines
T +33 (0)4 79 00 38 87
Route de Mussillon, 7am-12.30pm, 3-7.30pm.
Sells take-away pizzas.

Plateau

Maison Braissand Les Flocons
T +33 (0)4 79 00 54 23
Near the Casino supermarket

Méribel-Village
Village des pains
T +33 (0)4 79 08 59 26
Next to Lodge du Village, 7.30am-12.30pm, 4-7.30pm.

Offers a tempting selection of pastries and rustic breads as well as sandwiches, deli food and take-away pizzas. You can also hire raclette and fondue equipment here.

Butchers

In addition to the shops listed below, most of the supermarkets also sell meat.

Méribel
Boucherie Petit
T +33 (0)4 79 08 65 45
Route de Mussillon, next to the Casino supermarket, 8am-12.30pm, 3-7.30pm.

They have a good selection of meat, ready-prepared meals and spit-roasted chickens.

Plateau

Boucherie du Plateau
T +33 (0)4 79 08 60 53
Near the Casino supermarket.

Markets

On Fridays there is a market on Route de la Montée, running from the pharmacy to the Chaudanne. There are stalls selling local cheese, sausages and delicacies as well as cheap fleeces and ski jackets.

Newsagents and Tobacconists

You can buy UK newspapers in most newsagents. They also sell lots of useful things like phone cards, stamps and postcards. Not all sell tobacco goods – they will have a 'Tabac' sign outside if they do.

Méribel

Point Presse
The Chaudanne
Above Le Tremplin brasserie, 7.30am-7.30pm.

Maison de Presse
Route de Centre
In the Galerie des Cimes on the right-hand side of the road as you walk up the hill away from the tourist office, 9am-8pm (in low season may close over lunch).

A handy little shop with a wide selection of newspapers and magazines. Also sells sweets, toys and games.

Tabac des Cimes
Route de Centre
In the Galerie des Cimes, 9am-7.30pm.

Mottaret

Tabac La Mode des Montagnes
Near the main lift area, next to 'Au Temps Perdu' restaurant, 7am-7.30pm.

Les Allues

Tabac
Route de la Rèse
Near the supermarket, 7.30am-12.30pm, 4.30-7.30pm.

Skiing with **children**... dream or nightmare? With a little planning, it can be your best ski holiday ever.

What you'll find in this chapter

Accommodation	123
Childcare	127
Ski schools	127
Lift passes	127
Activities	130
Restaurants	131

Skiing can be a fantastic family holiday and Méribel has a lot to offer for children.

The resort is a member of 'Les p'tits Montagnards' club set up by Ski France to recognise child-friendly resorts. This takes into account areas such as medical facilities and child friendly restaurants (**> maddogski.com**).

Accommodation

Children love the social interaction of chalets and hotels, and childcare costs can usually be shared and are simple to arrange, especially through tour operators. On the other hand, self-catering arrangements are more flexible (particularly at meal times).

If you have young children, being close to the slopes, a bus stop or a ski locker is particularly important, as you will inevitably end up carrying their skis as well as your own!

Accommodation checklist

There are a number of questions you may want to ask when booking your holiday:

- Are there price reductions for children?
- Are cots, high chairs and baby monitors provided (or can they be hired)?
- Can extra beds be added into the parents' room?
- Are any other children booked into the chalet? How old are they?
- Are the children's rooms located away from the communal area (which can be noisy until late)?
- Are there baths available rather than just showers?
- Can the company provide nannies and/or babysitters or recommend someone local? What qualifications do they have and what is the adult to child ratio?

- Can high tea be arranged for the children?
- Is it a long or uphill walk to the slopes/nearest bus stop? If so, does the company provide a shuttle bus or lockers near the slopes?

Child-friendly tour operators

Many chalets and some hotels offer childcare, demand is usually high, especially in school holiday periods, so make sure you book as early as possible.

These companies have a great reputation for being family friendly.

Mark Warner

T +44 (0)870 770 4228
W markwarner.co.uk

Mark Warner's level of repeat business is testament to their commitment to families holidaying in the Alps. Clubs are run by trained nannies for children from four months upwards.

Crystal

T +44 (0)870 160 6040
W crystalski.co.uk

Crystal offer a wide range of accommodation, some with family rooms and free child places.

Meriski

T +44 (0)1285 648518
W meriski.co.uk

Chalet holidays with carefully considered arrangements for children. Care available either in the crèche or chalet for babies to six years old. The 'Merikids' club looks after children aged six to 12.

Purple Ski

T +44 (0)1885 488 799 (UK)
  +33 (0)4 79 01 05 31 (France)
W purpleski.com

Purple Ski has a choice of four chalets in the resort; one in Méribel, two in Mottaret and one in Méribel-Village. They offer childcare and babysitting services through a private nanny service.

Scott Dunn

Exceptional family ski holidays

The most important part of the family ski holiday formula is making sure the younger members of your group are happy. If they're happy you'll be happy.

We offer excellent childcare in all our alpine resorts - Courchevel 1850, Méribel, St Anton, Val d'Isère and Zermatt. And this year sees the launch of OurSpace, a dedicated winter children's club in Val d'Isère for our younger guests aged between 4 months and 13 years.

Having children does not mean the end of the adventure, if anything, as I'm sure you've realised, it is just the beginning.

Call our ski team now on **020 8682 5050**
or visit **www.scottdunn.com/ski**

Scott Dunn

T +44 (0)208 682 5000
W scottdunn.com

Luxury holidays, offering nannies, children's club and ski school. Thoughtful additions such as buying your baby's nappies make your holiday easier. They also give you an end of day report on your child's activities.

Ski Cuisine

T +44 (0)1702 589543
W skicuisine.co.uk

This company offers a chalet-based nanny service. All their nannies speak English and have a recognised qualification. Older children can be collected from ski school and looked after for the afternoon. Early supper provided on request.

Snowline
T +44 (0)844 557 3118
W snowline.co.uk
Private nanny service.

Supertravel
T +44 (0)207 295 1650
W supertravel.co.uk
Resort staff will drive your young ones to and from ski school and prepare meals for them. Nannies five days a week.

Hotels
If you prefer staying in a hotel then have a look at La Chaudanne (> 16) and Le Yéti (> 16). Both offer 3-star accommodation close to the piste.

Childcare
The tourist office can provide a list of English-speaking child minders and babysitters but you will need to check with the individual what their qualifications are.

Lift passes
Make the most of the Family Pass, with significant discounts on a six to 21 day holiday (minimum of four people; two adults and at least two children under 18).

Children under five have free lift passes (with proof of age and a photograph).

Ski school
Generally, children can start skiing from around the age of four and this is the earliest most schools will accept them. The stronger their leg muscles are, the easier they will find snow ploughs and the more fun they will have. Very young children (up to six) may only have the energy to do half a day on the slopes. The rest of the time might be better spent playing in the snow, or back in the resort (suggested activities > 130).

If your kids have fun they'll be hooked for life and the improvement will come so don't worry too much about technical progress.

Group or private lessons

British ski schools tend to offer smaller groups, where your kids can benefit from the social side of being in a class and the friendly interaction with other children makes this an ideal environment in which to learn. If you book ESF remember to request an English-speaking instructor. If you're taking lessons too, check that your meeting point is close to your children's for dropping them off and collecting them.

ESF ski school

T +33 (0)4 79 08 60 31 (Méribel)
T +33 (0)4 79 08 58 81 (Chaudanne)
T +33 (0)4 79 08 89 42 (Rond-Point)
T +33 (0)4 79 00 49 49 (Mottaret)
W esf-meribel.com

The main French ski school provides group lessons for children aged five to 13. Sunday or Monday start usually available. Prices include a pass to the Méribel valley. Beginners start around €190 for six mornings (slightly less for experienced skiers). You can also select afternoon-only or full-day classes. Request English-speaking instructors on booking.

Magic Academy

T +33 (0)4 79 08 53 36
W www.magic-meribel.com

International ski school, minimum age four, maximum group size six. Sunday and Monday starts usually available.

New Generation

T +33 (0)4 79 01 03 18
W www.skinewgen.com

Minimum age four, Sunday or Monday start, maximum group size eight (six for four and five year olds). Full morning lessons for six to twelve year olds > 33.

First day at ski school

- Write your contact number on a piece of paper and put it in your

- child's pocket
- Plenty of sun cream (water resistant and at least 30 SPF) is essential. Put the tube in their pocket so they can top up throughout the day
- Most schools insist that children wear ski helmets. You can hire these in resort
- Younger eyes are more sensitive so good sunglasses or goggles are important. If you only buy one, goggles are more versatile and less easy to lose
- Choose gloves or mittens your child can take on and off easily themselves; they'll have to do this numerous times throughout the day. (If possible, choose ones that attach to their clothing)

- Slightly older kids can use a small rucksack for carrying drinks, snacks and sun cream. Make sure they are careful not to catch them on chairlifts though
- Children lose body heat faster than adults so make sure they're wrapped up warmly
- If you're booking younger children into ski school, remember to give them a drink and snack for the mid-lesson break
- Even if your children are not in ski school, use sticky labels or band-aids to mark skis and helmets with their name as things are often thrown into a big bundle
- Complete beginners (especially little ones) will not need poles in ski lessons, at least at first
- Check if they need a lift pass or if it is included in the cost of lessons

Children's activities

These suggestions are particularly good for kids but also see **Other things to do** (> 107).

Bowling

A six-lane bowling alley complete with electronic boards, games and a bar is available at Parc Olympique. Pre-booking is advisable.

Ice skating

At the Parc Olympique from 2pm every afternoon (4pm on Wednesdays) until 7.30pm, late opening to 9.30pm on Tuesdays and Thursdays, children under five go free.

Sledging

Buy sledges and bum boards from most shops and supermarkets. The most popular sledging area for children is at Rond-Point, which also has a moving carpet. The Altiport is also suitable for sledging.

Older children looking for a challenge may want to take the luge run from Courchevel 1850 to 1550 (> 112).

Swimming

At the Parc Olympique, from 2-7.15pm (until 9.15pm on Tuesdays and Thursdays). A 25m pool, flume (for children over six) and baby pool.

Shopping

Most supermarkets stock baby food and formula but if you have any favourite products, it's best to bring them with you. Most ski shops stock children's sizes too so it's easy to replace any lost items. For toys try tabacs, the many gift shops and **Maison de Presse** on Route du Centre, near the cinema.

Restaurants

Restaurants in resort and on the mountain usually go out of their way to welcome children. Most offer simple dishes and some have children's menus or portions. We particularly like these places.

Méribel
La Galette
➤ 74
Pizza Express
➤ 75
Le Trempline
➤ 76

Mottaret
Au Temps Perdu
➤ 76

Mountain restaurants
The main problem on the mountain is the lunchtime queue. To avoid this, reserve a table or eat early (before 12.30pm). Service is usually quicker at self-service restaurants, or pack a picnic and enjoy the mountain views.

These are our favourites for families (other mountain restaurants ➤ 86).

Adray Télébar
➤ 93
Les Rhododendrons
➤ 93
Le Rond Point
➤ 95
Le Bel Air
➤ 97
Les Roc Tania
➤ 99
Le Chalet des 2 Lacs
➤ 105
Les Quatre Vents
➤ 102

MÉRIBEL®

CŒUR DES 3 VALLÉES

The list – it might sound boring but you'll find all the important information that you don't know you need till you need it...

Banks, bureau de change and cashpoints

Bank opening hours shown are Monday to Friday unless specified otherwise. All the banks have a cashpoint.

Méribel
Banque de Savoie
Main square, opposite Hotel le Roc. 8.50am-12pm, 2.20-6pm (5.15pm on Fridays).

Banque Populaire des Alpes
La Croix de Verdon, on the left-hand side as you come into Méribel's shopping area from Mussillon. 8.30am-12.15pm, 2.35-6.15pm.

Crédit Agricole
Route de la Montée, on the right-hand side as you head towards the Chaudanne, just past the pharmacy. 8.30am-12.00pm, 2.30-6.15pm.

Post Office ('La Poste')
Main square, next to the tourist office. 9am-12pm, 3-6pm (9.30am-12pm Saturdays).
Bureau de Change facilities available.

Mottaret
Crédit Agricole
In the main shopping area, by the Annexe Bar and Pizzeria du Mottaret.
Cashpoint only.

Méribel-Village
The Spar
8am-12.30pm, 4-7.30pm.
Has Bureau de Change services but no cashpoint.

Buses
In resort
'Meribus' runs free shuttle buses between the different levels of the resort. In the centre of Méribel, the bus stops you are most likely to use are at the Chaudanne (located outside the Parc Olympique, across the road from Le Tremplin brasserie) and by Hotel Le Roc (this stop is indicated on timetables as 'Méribel O.T' – Office du Tourisme). For other stops, look for the 'Arrêt Navette' or 'Arrêt Bus' signs and remember to wait on the correct side of the road.

The four main routes from Méribel are set out below (times given indicate the approximate length of travel from the Chaudanne bus stop):
- the Altiport via the Rond-Point (20 and 15 minutes respectively)
- Le Hameau via Mottaret (20 and 10 minutes respectively)
- the Belvédère area (20 minutes)
- Les Allues via Méribel Village (20 and 10 minutes respectively)

Bus frequency varies for each route; pick up a timetable from the tourist office when you arrive. Bus information is available from Meribus on +33 (0)4 79 08 53 66 or the tourist office on +33 (0)4 79 08 60 01.

During peak periods the buses can get very crowded and there have been complaints that they aren't frequent enough. To limit your reliance on, you can rent a piste-side ski locker to store your skis and boots in overnight and walk home.

Further afield

A limited early evening bus service runs from Mottaret via the Méribel tourist office to La Tania, Le Praz, Courchevel 1650 and Courchevel 1850. The full journey from Mottaret to Courchevel 1850 takes just under an hour and costs €9 one way. For information on this and other routes from Méribel contact **Transavoie** on +33 (0)4 79 08 54 90 (Méribel) or +33 (0)4 79 00 42 39 (Méribel-Mottaret) **altibus.com.** Alternatively contact the tourist office.

For getting to and from airports and train stations > 18.

Car hire

For information on car hire from airports > 18.

There are garages in Méribel which partner international hire companies and/or have their own vehicles. All companies listed below have English-speaking staff and, if you're planning on hiring a car while in the resort, we recommend speaking to them about prices and availability before you leave home:

Méribel
Garage Alp Auto,
T +33 (0)4 79 00 59 60
Mussillon (next to Dicks Tea Bar).
Méribel Garage,
T +33 (0)4 79 00 45 27,
Mussillon.
Mottaret
Garage Breton
T +33 (0)4 79 00 42 84

Car parks
See map > 6.

Cashpoints
See **banks** > 132.

Catering and support services
Chaletfood
T +33 (0)6 13 56 41 73
W chaletfood.com
Pre-order your shopping before you leave the UK and it will be delivered to your accommodation when you arrive.

Prestige Services
T +33 (0)4 67 28 09 62
or +33 (0)6 07 40 75 12
W prestigeservices.eu.com
Cooking services for those in self-catered accommodation. The company will also carry out administrative tasks such as arranging your ski pass.

Churches
Eglise St Martin in Les Allues
T +33 (0)4 79 08 61 03
W chez.com/martinallues
Regular Roman Catholic services (free shuttle bus from Méribel provided). For up-to-date information and times see the 'Highlights of the week' leaflet from the tourist office or contact the church direct. The leaflet also contains details on Protestant and Anglican services in the region.

Cinema
> 108.

Cleaning
Boutik Services Méribel
T +33 (0)6 30 35 53 39
Apartment cleaning services.

Consulate

British Consulate
T +33 (0)4 72 77 81 70
24 rue Childebert, 69002 Lyon
Monday to Friday 9am-12.30pm,
2-5pm.

For emergencies outside those hours contact the duty officer on +33 (0)4 72 77 81 78.

Credit cards
Payment by credit card is commonplace although many French establishments do not accept American Express. When using your debit or credit card, most places require a PIN number.

Dentist

M. Pomagalski
T +33 (0)4 79 08 67 61
Medical centre in the Parc Olympique at the Chaudanne. By appointment only.

Doctor
> 138.

Electricity
France operates on a 220 volts/50hz ac. system. Most UK appliances should work but you'll need a two-pin adaptor.

Emergency numbers
Fire Brigade:
18 (112 from mobile phones)
Medical Emergency: 15
Police:
+33 (0)4 79 08 60 17 or 17
Need emergency numbers in a hurry? See the inside front cover of this guide.

Events
'Welcome to Méribel' (Bienvenue à Méribel), a booklet of seventy-odd pages produced by the tourist office every season, lists the resort's main events. A more detailed breakdown, including cinema listings, sporting spectacles and live music, is set out in the Office's free leaflet 'Highlights of the Week' (Les Coups de Coeur). Both documents are published in French and English and are distributed throughout the resort as well as by the tourist offices. Other good sources of information

The Environment

There is always a tremendous amount of rubbish on the slopes when the snow melts – don't add to it. A single cigarette butt contains 4,000 toxic substances and can pollute up to 1.3 m³ of snow – under any one chairlift there could be up to 30,000 butts.

How long does rubbish last?
Plastic bottle: 100 – 1000 years
Aluminium cans: 100 – 500 years
Cigarette stubs: 2 – 7 years
Fruit peel: 3 days – 6 months
Sweet wrappers: 100 – 450 years

Source: mountain-riders.org

The Ski Club of Great Britain is running a campaign to safeguard the environment and the long-term future of skiing. See **respectthemountain.com** for details.

are the tourist office website (meribel.net), posters around the resort and notice boards in local bars.

Garages
Petrol is available from the Elan garage between Les Allues and Méribel. Petrol in Moûtiers is cheaper than in the resort – try Agip or Elf as you leave Moûtiers heading towards resort.

Hairdressers
See Beauty and therapies > 107.

Health

See also Medical (> 138).

A few tips to keep you healthy on holiday:

- The sun is much stronger at altitude – make sure you wear sun cream even on overcast days
- You need to drink at least three times as much water to keep hydrated at altitude – more if you're topping up with wine and beer. Your muscles are the first part of your body to dehydrate so you'll suffer less aches and pains if you keep hydrated
- Good sunglasses are a must to prevent watering eyes and snow blindness
- Lip salve with a high sun-protection factor will prevent unattractive chapped lips
- If there's a lot of icy weather around, some sports shops sell 'Gliss Pas' soles for your shoes – makes walking on icy pavements less hazardous

Internet

A number of cafés and bars offer broadband internet access – charges vary but expect to pay around €4 per half hour. Check if there are restrictions on when you can use the computers as certain establishments don't offer it at lunchtime or during peak après-ski time. Some of the places to try are listed below:

Méribel

Cactus Café
T +33 (0)4 79 00 53 67
By the Chaudanne.
8am-midnight.

Cybar at La Taverne
T *+33 (0)4 79 00 36 18*
Main Square, beneath Hotel Le Roc, 7.30am-1am.

Scott's Bar
T +33 (0)4 79 00 39 61
Main Square, to the right of the tourist office 4pm-1.30 am.

Le Rond-Point
T +33 (0)4 79 00 37
By the Rond-Point bus stop, 51, 12–6pm.

maddogski.com

Tourist office
T +33 (0)4 79 08 60 01
Main square, 9am-7pm.

Mottaret
Tourist office
T +33 (0)4 79 00 42 34
Large wooden building in the main lift area, 9am-7pm.

Les Allues
La Tsaretta
T +33 (0)4 79 08 61 00
Route des Carons opposite the church, from 5pm.

Language

Although many of the people working in shops and restaurants speak English, a little French goes a long way. Don't be discouraged if they answer you back in English – the fact that you spoke French to them will usually make a difference. See our useful phrases over the page.

Laundrette
Laverie Pingouin'net
at the Chaudanne (near Hotel Grangettes), 8.30am-9.30pm.
Self-service.

Massage
See Beauty and therapies > 107.

Medical
Ambulance +33 (0)4 79 55 28 67.
In an emergency dial 15.

Doctors and medical centres
Méribel
T +33 (0)4 79 08 60 41
Medical Centre Parc Olympique, 9.30am-7pm.

1600
T +33 (0)4 79 08 65 40
Medical Centre 'Altitude 1600', 9am-7pm.

Mottaret
T +33 (0)4 79 00 40 88
Centre Commercial 'Le Ruitor', 9.30am-6.30pm.

1600
British chartered physiotherapy clinic
T +33 (0)6 68 57 00 98
Near Chez Kiki restaurant.
By appointment only, home visits also available.

Meeting rooms
There are rooms available to rent for meetings in the Parc Olympique Sport Centre at the Chaudanne. Contact the centre for details.

Optician
Méribel
Cimes Optique
T +33 (0)4 79 00 52 77
La Croix de Verdon, first shop on the left as you come into Méribel's shopping area from Mussillon, 10am-12.30pm, 3-7pm.

Méribel Optic
T +33 (0)4 79 00 37 88
By the Chaudanne, 9am-12.30pm, 3.30-7.15pm.

Parking
See map ➤ 6.

Pharmacy
Méribel
T +33 (0)4 79 08 63 59
Route de la Montée, on the right-hand side as you head from Hotel Le Roc to the Chaudanne, 8.45am-12.30pm, 3.30-5.15 pm.

Mottaret
T +33 (0)4 79 00 43 70
In the main shopping centre, next to Pizzaria du Mottare, 9.30am-6.30pm.

Photography
Méribel
Adventure Photo
T +33 (0)4 79 00 46 04
Route de la Montée, on the left-hand side as you head from Hotel Le Roc to the Chaudanne, just before Grand Marnier Crêpes, 9am-12.30pm, 2.30-7.30 pm.
One-hour developing available.

The list

maddogski.com

Useful phrases:	
Hello	Bonjour
Goodbye	Au revoir
How are you?	Comment ça va?
Please	S'il vous plait
Thank-you	Merci
Excuse me/sorry	Excusez-moi
How much…?	C'est combien?
The bill please	L'addition, s'il vous plait
Jug of tap water	Un carafe d'eau
Snowboard	Snowboard
Skis	Les skis
Ski/boarding boots	Chaussures des ski/surf ski/boarding boots
Ski poles	Batons
Lift pass	Forfait
I am lost	Je suis perdu
Where is the nearest lift/restaurant?	Ou est le télésiège/restaurant le plus près?
Help!	Au secours!
Watch out!	Attention!

Piste information

Méribel

T +33 (0)4 79 08 65 32
Méribel Alpina.
run an information hut in the centre of the Chaudanne,

Mottaret

T +33 (0)4 79 00 88 60
S3V
offers information from the tourist office.

Physiotherapists

See also Medical (> 138).

Police

T +33 (0)4 79 08 60 17 or 17.

Post Offices ('La Poste') and post boxes

There is no need to go to the Post Office to buy stamps; most places selling postcards will also sell stamps to the UK. Post boxes are pale yellow and usually fixed to the wall rather than free standing.

Méribel

T +33 (0)4 79 08 61 69
Main Square (next to the tourist office), 9am-12pm, 3-6pm weekdays and 9.30am-12pm Saturdays.
The closest post box to the Chaudanne is to your right as you stand facing Méribel Optic opticians on Route de la Montée.

Mottaret

T +33 (0)4 79 00 40 26
Weekdays only, in the tourist office building, 9am-12pm, 3-5.30pm.

Radio

Radio R'Méribel 97.9 and 98.9 fm. Broadcasts each day between 7.30am-10am and 5-7pm. English information (news and forecasts) are given between 8-9am and after 6pm.

Rubbish

Look out for the *'Abri Poubelle'* signs on small wooden huts around the resort. The huts keep the bins snow-free and the animals away. Many also contain recycling bins with clear signs to tell you what can go in each bin.

Safety

Ski resorts are traditionally a safe place to holiday. Most crime involves theft so ensure you keep your belongings with you in the bar and also keep your accommodation locked at all times.

To protect your skis from thieves, you should get into the habit of swapping skis with your companions so you leave mismatched pairs outside restaurants and bars.

Shops
> 115.

Ski lockers
If your accommodation is some way from the slopes, you may want to think about renting a locker to store your skis and boots in. Lockers accommodate up to three sets of skis / boots and cost €10 per day or €41 for six days plus a deposit of €10. Sharing is easy as you are given three keys. The lockers are located at the Chaudanne by the lift entrance marked 'Télécabine de Burgin / Saulire'.

T +33 (0)4 79 08 65 32
8.45am-5.45pm.

Taxis
Taxis are not that expensive and are a convenient way to get around the resort. The main taxi rank in the centre of Méribel is at the top of Route de la Montée, across the road from La Taverne and Hotel Le Roc. In Mottaret it's near the tourist office building.

Most taxi firms offer services from airports and train stations, although this is not usually the cheapest route. If you're making a longer journey, some firms have websites listing their fares so you can compare prices before you book. There are numerous firms operating in the resort including:

G'Taxi
T +33 (0)6 09 52 78 52
W gtaximeribel.com

Méritaxis
T +33 (0)4 79 08 58 22
W meri-taxis.com

Taxi Jean Loup
T +33 (0)6 09 44 15 95
W taxijeanloup.com

Taxiphone Méribel
T +33 (0)4 79 08 65 10

Taxiphone Méribel-Mottaret
T +33 (0)4 79 00 44 29

Telephones

Although most people tend to use their mobile, there are public telephones throughout the resort. Télécartes can be bought from tabacs and newsagents. Prices start from €7.50.

Time

French time is GMT +1 hour.

Tipping

Restaurants and bars: tip up to a couple of euros. If it's very 'luxe', the tip should reflect the service.

Instructors: if you enjoyed your week of lessons, tip your instructor €10-15 each.

Chalet hosts: most survive the season on next to nothing. If yours make a positive difference to your holiday, they will not be offended by a cash gift at the end of the week. If you had good service, you should tip at least €10-15 per adult guest – more for exceptional service.

Toilets
Méribel
In the tourist office and at the Chaudanne (in Télécabine de Tougnète building).

Mottaret
Downstairs in the tourist office.

Tourist offices

The offices are well equipped and have toilets and photo booths.

Méribel
T +33 (0)4 79 08 60 01
Main square, next to the Post Office, 9am-7pm.

Mottaret
T +33 (0)4 79 00 42 34
In the large wooden building in the main lift area, 9am-7pm.

The tourist office is a great source of useful information. It's also worth having a look at their website (meribel.net) before you arrive. Once in the resort, we recommend picking up the following:
- A bus timetable
- The 'Welcome to Méribel' *(Bienvenue a Méribel)* booklet. It lists various shops and services and has resort maps in the back

The list

maddogski.com

- The 'Highlights of the Week' *(Les Coups de Coeur)* leaflet is filled with live music events, sporting activities and films taking place in the resort.

Trains

The nearest train station is in Moûtiers, which is about 18 kilometres from the resort.

If you want train information while at the resort you can contact SNCF on +33 (0)4 79 00 53 28, voyages-sncf.com. Alternatively ask at the Méribel tourist office +33 (0)4 79 08 60 01.

Weather

Generally you can expect January and February to be colder than March and April. December has less snow but can be cheaper, except around Christmas and New Year. Members of the **Ski Club of Great Britain** can obtain historical snow reports from their website (skiclub.co.uk).
The following provide current weather forecasts:
- **maddogski.com** weather forecasts and webcams
- **Méribel Flash**
  T +33 (0)8 92 30 33 02 (€0.34 per minute) – daily information on weather and risk alerts.
- **meteo.fr/montagne**
  T +33 (0)8 92 68 02 73 (€0.34 per minute) – three-day forecasts with snowfall, temperature and wind information.

Index

A

Accommodation	14, 123
Activities	107
Adray Télébar	93
Airlines	17
Airports	17
transfers to/from	14, 19
Les Allues	10
L'Alpage	100
L'Altibar, Le Pilatus	95
L'Altiself 3000	103
Annexe bar	84
Après-ski	79
L'Arc-en-ciel	95
L'Arpasson	93
Au Temps Perdu	76
Avalanche	30

B

Babysitters	127
Bakers	120
Banks	132
Le Bar de la Marine	104
Baromoter	80
Bars	79
Beauty	107
Beginner slopes	27
Le Bel Air	97
Le Blanchot	95
Boarders	26
Board hire	34
Le Bouc Blanc	98
La Bouitte	100
Bowling	108
Brasserie Le Tremplin	76
Budget restaurants	69
Bureau de change	132
Buses	18, 132
Butchers	120

C

Cactus Cafe	73, 81
Le Cap Horn	95
Car hire	18, 133
Car parks	134
Cashpoints	132
La Casserole	98
Le Chalet des 2 Lacs	105
Le Chalet de 2 Ours	104
Le Chalet du Cairn	100
Le Chalet de Caron	104
Le Chalet de Chavière	104
Le Chalet du Génépi	105
Le Chalet des Neiges	100
Le Chalet de Pierres	96
Le Chalet Plein Sud	106
Le Chalet Refuge	
Le Chalet du Thorens	105
Le Chalet Togniat	94
Chalets	16
Le Chardon Bleu	99

Le Chardonnet............................ 94
Les Chenus 96
Chez From'ton 73
Chez Kiki 73
Childcare 127
Children.................................... 123
Chinal Donat........................... 105
Les Choucas 93
Churches 134
Cigarettes 122
Cinema 108
Climbing 110
Le Corbeleys 99
Côte 2000.................................. 94
Crèche...................................... 127
Credit cards 135
Les Crêtes.................................. 93
La Croix Jean-Claude 77
Le Cro Magnon 73
Cross-country skiing 26

Cuisine 66
Currency 2

D

Day trips 54
Delicatessens 118
Dentist..................................... 135
Dick's Tea bar 82
Doctor 138
Driving...................................... 19

E

Emergency numbers 135
Les Enfants Terribles............... 74
Environment 136
Equipment hire 34
L'Etape 3200 106
Events 114, 135
Evolution 74

F

Families................................... 123
La Flambee 74
Fifty50 82
Flights 110
Food and drink 66, 118
Foreign exchange 132
Le France aka Chez Alfred 101

G

La Galette 74
Garages 136
Grand Marnier Crepes 75
Go-karting.............................. 110
Le Grand Lac 101
Le Grenier................................ 77
Guided tours 113

H

Hairdressers 136
Health 137

Heli-skiing 26	Live music 80	Mountain guides 26
Hospital 138	Lockers 142	Mountain restaurants 86
Hot air balloon 110	Lodge du Village 77, 84	La Moutière 106
Hotels 16	Le Loft 83	Music 80
	La Loy 100	
I	Luge/sledging 112	**N**
Ice skating 110		Nannies 127
Insurance 20	**M**	Newsagents 122
Internet access 137	Mad Dog – contact us 1	Newspapers 122
	Maps	Nightlife 79
J	*mountain restaurants* 87	Non-skiing activities 107
Jack's Bar 82	*piste* 87	Nurseries 127
	restaurant and bar 72	
K	*village* 6	**O**
Kids 123	Massage 108	Off-licence 118
	Méribel	Off-piste 26
L	*introduction to* 5	Optician 139
Language 138	*village* 9	L'Ours Blanc 98
Lift opening/closing times 29	Le Mont de la Chambre 102	
Lift passes 27	Motteret 8	

maddogski.com

P

Paintballing 110
Le Panoramic 97, 102
Paragliding 110
Parking 6
Pharmacy 139
Photography 139
Physiotherapist 139
Les Pierres Plates 94
Pizzeria de Mottaret 77
Pizza Express 75
Picnics 69
Les Pierres Plates 94
Piste map 87
Piste ranking 34
Police 140
Le Poste 83
Post Office 141
Le Privilege 84
Le Pub 83
Pub Le Ski Lodge 99

Q

Les Quatre Vents 102

R

Le Refuge 75
Restaurants 73
Resort:
    Les Allues 10
    Méribel 8
    Méribel Mottaret 8
    Méribel-Village 9
Mountain:
    Méribel 23
    Courchevel 24
    St Martin 24
    Les Menuires 24
    Val Thorens 24
Les Rhododendrons 93
Le Roc des 3 Marches 102
Le Roc Tania 99
Les Roches Blanches 103

Rond Point 83, 95
La Ruade 101

S

Safety 31, 141
Saunas 107
Scott's 76, 84
Self-catering 16
Shopping 115
La Sitelle 94
Ski area 23
    guiding 27
    hire 33
    kit 35
    day trips 54
    school 32
    children's 127
Skidoos 111
Sledging 112
Snowboard 26

hire	34
Snow reports	3
Snow shoe hiking	113
Snowparks	26
Les Sonnailles	101
La Soucoupe Restaurant	97
Spas	107
Supermarkets	118
Swimming	114
Symbols, guide to	70.79

T
Take-aways	69
La Taverne	76, 84
Taxis	119, 42
Telephones	143
Toilets	143
Tourist offices	143
Trains	144
Transfers	19
Le Tsaretta	78, 85

U
| Using this book | 2 |

V
Vegetarians	68
Les Verdons	97
Villages	8

W
| Walks | 113 |
| Weather | 144 |

maddogski.com

And finally...

We would like to thank the following people for their help and support: Susie Aust, Matt Bird, Phillip Blackwell, Juliet Clay, Carrie Hainge at the Ski Club of Great Britain, Penny Harding, Paddi Hutchins-Clarke, Juliet Johnston, Simon Milton, Louise Moore.

Photo credits

Meribel tourist office – P5, 28, 33, 55, 62, 63, 78, 86, 126, 129, 132.
Divider – About Mad Dog, About Meribel, Planning your trip, On the piste, Other things to do, Children
Pascal Leroy – P103
Robyn Mackenzie – P64

Nicolae Popovici – P121
Par Soderman – P85
Colin Soutar - P
Divider – Food and drink
iStock – P22, 92, 96
Kate Whittaker – P70

Do you know something we don't? Jot down your tips and recommendations and let us know about them at info@maddogski.com

---

Do you know something we don't? Jot down your tips and recommendations and let us know about them at info@maddogski.com